NEW PREDICTIVE ASTROLOGY

NEW PREDICTIVE ASTROLOGY

DR. R.N. VYAS

GYAN PUBLISHING HOUSE
NEW DELHI - 110002

NEW PREDICTIVE ASTROLOGY
(Astrology)

ISBN : 81-212-0685-5

Published in 2000 in India by
Gyan Publishing House
5, Ansari Road
New Delhi 110 002
Laser Typesetting: Grow Computers, Delhi.
Printed at Mehra Offset Press, New Delhi.

Something is not good only because it is old. Nor anything is bad because it is new. Prudent persons test everything logically and rationally and accept it on the basis of its merit. Unintelligent persons accept anything only because it has been accepted by others.

— Kalidasa

Ring out the old, ring in the new,
Ring, happy bells, across the snow:
The year is going, let him go;
Ring out the false, ring in the true.

—Tennyson

How longsoever it hath continued, if it be against reason, it is of no force in law.

—Sir Edward Coke

सूर्याद् भवन्ति भूनानि सूर्येण पार्लनानि
सुनछु भरम भावी प्रबल, विलखि कहे मुनिनाथ
हानि लाभ जीवन मरण दश अध्याय विधि हाथ

CONTENTS

Appendices

PREFACE

By nature man is inquisitive. The prime aim of one's inquisitiveness is to know one's own future, the events that shall mark one's future life.

The famous Upanishadic declaration says *Atmanam Viddhi*. Shora of its philosophical connotation, it only means 'Let me know my future'.

This inquisitiveness is so deeprooted in man that astrology, which is a science of knowing future events, appears to be as old as man. Jyotisha (astrology) is one of the parts of the Vedas (Vedanga). But future is unseen *(adrishta)*. All attempts to know the future merely mean attempts of knowing possibilities. Certainty is a divine virtue. No mortal man can assert it. Even modern physics now talks about mere possibilities or probabilities.

Unfortunately, some people consider astrology as a science of judging exactly what is going to happen. This tendency has brought ridicule to astrology. It has been condemnded as superstition.

Let me quote here Voltaire, the French thinker, who flourished in 18th century. What he said then about astrology, is true even now. He wrote in his Philosophical History:

"Astrology may rest on better foundation than magic. For if no one has seen either Geblins, or Lemures, or Dives, or Peris, or Demos, or Cacodemons, the predictions of astrologers have often been seen to succeed. If two astrologers were consulted on the life of a child and if, one says that the child will live to manhood, the other not; if one announces rain, and the other fine weather, it is clear that one of them will be a prophet.............

"I have not the honour of being a prince; but the celebrated count of Boulainvilliers and an Italian, named Colonne, who had much prestige in Paris, both foretold that I should die infallibly at the age of thirty-two. I have been so malicious as to deceive them already by nearly thirty years, wherefore I humbly beg their pardon." Even now we shall come across some persons who will like to have this type of disbelief in astrology.

But on the other hand there may be many other persons who have a sense of praise for astrology, because it gave them guidance and courage in the hour of sorrow and despondence.

The faith of people in astrology has increased all the more. The truth that one expects from astrology comes from the intuitive faculty of an astrologer which is aroused by astrological calculations. Without going deep into the matter, we can say that the average person likes to consult astrology.

The present work aims at simplifying, rationalizing and making it concise to the extent that a common man can have predictions at his own place without consulting any astrologer.

Special features have been included in this book keeping an average reader in mind, these are as follows:

1. Giving sole importance to Surya Kundali.
2. Disposing off Chandra Kundali, Navamasha, etc., totally.
3. Giving a new and fixed system of Mahadasha.
4. Asserting that astrology can yield merely possibilities and probability. Certainty is out of question.
5. Giving only essential information about the nature of planets (grahas) and Rashis.
6. Giving the effects of the planets in the twelve lagnas.

The work has been specially written for the common man to enable him to unearth the hidden possibilities of his life to a limited extent. The author hopes that the reader shall find it very convenient and useful. Even the problem of determining Chandra Rashi on the basis of name has been left out. This makes the work easiest for use. Astrology being a totally pragmatic science, academic discussions have little importance for a layman.

I thank the publisher for publishing the work in such a short time.

Academy House
17/2, North Rajmohalla,
Indore - 452002

R.N. Vyas

PART I

POSITION OF GRAHA AND LAGNA IN ASTROLOGY

1

SURYA'S IMPORTANCE FOR ASTROLOGY

In view of the extreme importance of Surya, it is better to be guided by Surya Rashi alone, as indicated in this work. It is easy and rational.

One has to take Surya Rashi as the Lagna Rashi and place the rest of the planets in the way they are placed in the Panchang (almanac) and know the result as indicated in this work.

Is it not very easy? One need not go to any astrologer. Of course, if one wants to do so, one can always do so. But for a broad astrological indication, this work is surely a good guide.

When the horoscope has been thus prepared, one can keep it with oneself and can judge the result from time to time along with the effects of transitions of planets. Planets keep on moving. But their influence can be judged by a person on the basis of their changing effects in one's horoscope along with their positions in the original horoscope.

Aspects of Planets

Aspects of the planets are very important in judging any horoscope. The rules of aspects can be gathered from the following account. All planets aspect their 7th house fully, e.g., if Surya is in Mesha its aspect will be on the 7th house, i.e., on Tula. This rule applies to all planets.

In addition to this rule which is applicable to all the planets, some planets have additional aspects.

Mangala aspects the 4th and 8th houses.

Guru aspects 5th and 9th houses.

Shani aspects 3rd and 10th houses.

These are major aspects and must be taken into account while judging any horoscope, both in the original horoscope as well as transition of planets.

Let me repeat that Surya occupies the most important position not only in Indian astrology but even in Indian thought as a whole. I have added one appendix to this work on the significance of Surya. That will make the matter clear.

Suryousnishad Declares

"Surya produces beings and maintains them. In the end all are lost in Surya and that Surya is my Being."

The term Surya is derived from a word that says that Surya makes the world beautiful.

Savita is another name of Surya. The term Savita means the originator of the world.

According to Indian calculations, Surya moves in different Rashis in the following order:

Date	*Rashi*
14th January	Makara
13th February	Kumbha
14th March	Meena
13th April	Mesha
14th May	Vrishabha
14th June	Mithuna
16th July	Karka
16th August	Simha
16th September	Kanya
14th October	Tula
16th November	Vrishchika
15th December	Dhanu

2

START FROM SURYA LAGNA

In the present mathodology which is being explained in this work one has to start from the preparation of the Lagna, i.e., the first house. A horoscope begins from the first house and concludes with the 12th house to be counted in the way mentioned herein below.

Determination of the Lagna is easy. It has to be fixed with the position of the Surya which is given in every Panchang. If the Surya is in Mesha, it will be Mesha Lagna, if the Surya is in Vrishabha, it will be Vrishabha Lagna, one should proceed in this manner. Thus there will be twelve possible Lagnas as there are twelve Rashis, viz., Mesha, Vrishabha, Mithuna, Karka, Simha, Kanya, Tula, Vrishchik, Dhanu, Makara, Kumbha, and Meena.

Owners of the Rashis:

Rashi	*Owner*
Mesha and Vrishchika	Mangal
Vrishabha and Tula	Shukra
Mithun and Kanya	Budha
Karka	Chandrama or Chandra
Simha	Surya
Makara and Kumbha	Shani
Dhanu and Meena	Guru
X	Rahu
X	Ketu

The twelve houses of a horoscope have specific significance shown as follows:

1. Body, 2. Dhana or riches, 3. Brothers, 4. Domestic Happiness,5. Sons or progeny, 6. Enemies, 7. Wife, 8. Death,

9. Dharma or morality or religion; 10. Karma or activity or nature of work, 11. Labha or gain, 12. Vyaya or expenditure.

This can be indicated through the following chart:

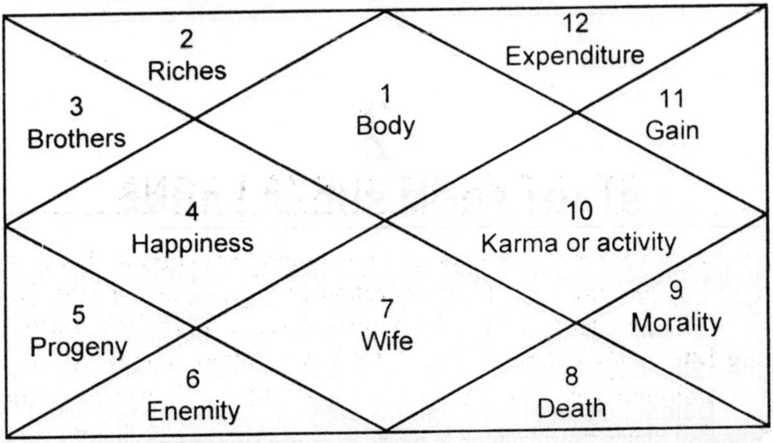

There are only nine planets and only twelve Rashis. Their nature shall be explained in this very work later on. However, classification of planets (grahas) according to their nature is as follows:

Grahas	*Nature*	*Broad Indications*
Surya, Chandra, Guru	Satvic	Knowledge, virtue, happiness
Budha, Shukra	Rajasic	Attachment, clinging
Mangal, Shani, Rahu, Ketu	Tamasic	Slowth, laziness

Indian astrology is a study of nine planets viz. Surya, Chandra, Mangal, Budha, Guru, Shukra, Shani, Rahu and Ketu and their placings in twelve Rashis viz. Mesha, Vrishabha, Mithuna, Kerka, Simha, Kanya, Tula, Vrishchik, Dhanu, Makara, Kumbha and Meena.

3

NECESSITY OF EASIER ASTROLOGY

Astrology is as old as the hills. Despite opposition by many persons, it has been attracting people from the time immemorial. Even in the present age of science, a big bulk of humanity has faith in it and consults it at least in an hour of suffering and confusion.

Personally I think that astrology which is practised by diehard Pundits needs certain modifications to make it suitable for the common man. At the hands of the priests and professionals, it has become a tainted and complicated means of livelihood. Many professionals use astrology for producing fear in the minds of the consulting people and persuade them to perform many pujas to placate some planets like Shani or Mangal, Rahu or Ketu. I know some astrologers who actually changed the horoscopes of some girls to see that they match with those boys with whom their matrimonial alliances were intended.

Astrology cannot escape this misuse as long as it remains encaged in the hands of some professionals. I know of some astrologers who actually terrorized some persons (customers) and accepted huge amount of money by promising to set the evil planets right through their Puja devices.

I therefore propose to present in this book astrology in a very simple form so that it may be used by any person of average intelligence and understanding with the help of some Panchang.

Of course, it does not intend to dissuade a person from a deeper study of the subject. A deeper study shall definitely prove beneficial as it may enable a person to have an indepth knowledge. Ordinarily, astrology is sought for common practical problems which can be handled by some easily gained knowledge too. Astrology is after all a science indicating certain possibilities. It should not be taken as a vehicle of absolutely certain knowledge of the coming events.

Traditional Indian astrology uses many charts like Janma Chakra, Chalit Chakra. Navamamnsha Chakra, Bhava Spashta, Graha Spashta Dasha Varga, Ashtaka Varga, Dasha, Mahadasha, etc. Of course, all these have their importance. But all these details make traditional astrology very complicated and beyond the reach of a common man.

Hence, we need an astrological system which is comparatively easier and simpler in practice. If it can act as a rough guide, the purpose of astrology will be served.

I intend to place in this book astrology shorn of complexities. Life runs smoothly ordinarily even without any help of astrology. But there are moments when one is terribly upset or perplexed for despondent. Astrological help may be sought in such conditions. A simple astrological method can be used by any average person with profit. Moreover, one is usually inquisitive about one's future. This inquisitiveness too may lead a person to consult astrology.

There is a Sanskrit statement which goes as follows:

Vanam smashrita ye'pi nirmama nishparigrahah

api te pariprichchanti jyotisham gatikovidam

Even the persons who have retired to the forest and have tried to free themselves from attachment and envy and have no worldly possessions, try to know their future. If an ordinary person tries to know his future through astrology, then it is but natural.

Let us take a simple example.

Mr. Paresh is blessed with a baby girl at 9.45 a.m. on 14.4.1998. He is naturally interested in knowing the fortune of the daughter roughly.

According to the system suggested in this work, he can do so rather easily. What he shall have to do is to see the position of Surya on that day and cast the horoscope on that basis.

Let us try to do so.

Birth Chart

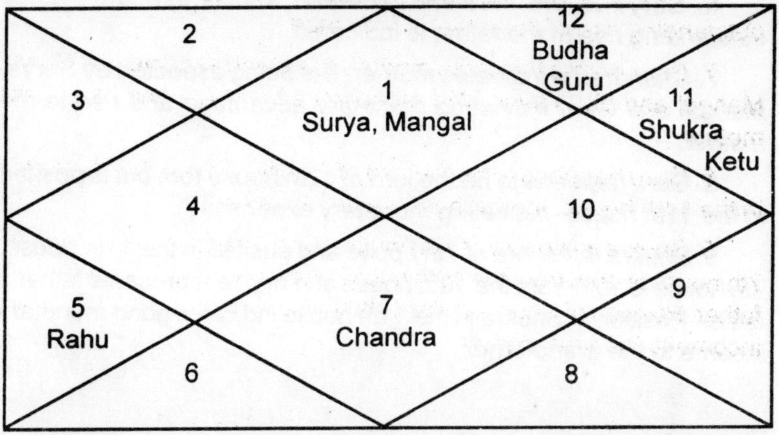

Why have we chosen Surya? It is because of the fact that Surya happens to be the most important planet. All other planets just move around it and derive energy from it.

Our rough reading of the above chart will be as stated below:

1. Lagna lord is posited in the Lagna along with Surya. Hence birth must have taken place through an operation.

2. There is a combination of Mangal and Surya, Surya being in its exalted position and Mangal being the lord of the Lagna Rashi itself. Surya is the lord of the 5th house. Hence the child shall prove to be an outstanding personality. Aspects of Guru, Shukra and Ketu on the 5th house are good. But presence of Rahu in the 5th house indicates that the person shall have free will and may not follow traditions slavishly.

3. Chandra represents mind. Chandra is in Tula, indicating a balanced temperament. It is being aspected by Guru making the person religious minded. The lord of 2nd and the 7th house is in the 11th in a friendly sign indicating good income. Shukra happens to be the lord of 2nd house too. Hence, there shall be good income of the family after her birth.

4. The lord of the 9th house is in the 11th house, indicating good fortune yielding good money.

5. Chandra is being aspected by Mangal and Surya too. This aspect indicates that the person shall be courageous and fearless and shall give utmost importance to self-respect.

6. Surya is the indicator of father and is exalted. Hence outstanding rise of the father is indicated.

7. Chandrama indicates mother. It is being aspected by Surya, Mangal and Guru indicating monetary advantage and rise to the mother.

8. Guru happens to be the lord of 12th house too, but is posited in the 11th house, indicating monetary expenses.

9. Shukra is the lord of 7th house and posited in the 11th house. 7th house is 10th from the 10th house and hence represents father's father. Position of Shukra in the 11th house indicates good monetary income to the grandfather.

4

NEED FOR MODIFICATION

Astrology is an ancient science which is as old as the Vedic period. Modifications of the system have been made from time to time either openly or secretly. The old order changes yielding place to new. Means of fast communications like railways, buses, aeroplanes, newspapers, radios, televisions, etc., have shrunken the world. Spatial distance has been much shortened. Social distance has been reduced. The world has developed willingly or unwillingly a sense of unity at least in the event of destruction and even in cooperation. Of course, things that disturb us even now do happen. Fundamentalism, narrow nationalism, terrorism, etc., have assumed larger dimensions. But we can hope that some day in the near future, even these problems shall be reduced in dimension if not uprooted totally. Indian astrology too has changed. I remember the days when solar and lunar eclipses were considered as the occasions of utmost puritanism. Now nobody seems to bother about it.

If we look at Panchangas, we find many *muhurtas* like Vadhu Pravesh Muhurta, Dwiragamana Muhurta, Pratham Yuvati Strisangama Muhurta, Muhurta for preparation of food by a newly wed daughter-in-law, Muhurta for going to father's house from husband's house, Muhurta for wearing ornaments and many others. One used to consult Muhurta for every act of going out, or shaving. In fact astrology used to govern every important and unimportant act of a person.

Now, nobody bothers about all this.

The ceremony of thread wearing and marriage too have undergone transformation. Thread ceremony has almost become obsolete and marriages are being performed even in the law courts.

I think that we should effect a change in the scheme of Mahadasha too.

At present Mahadasha runs in Indian astrology in the following order:

1. Surya dasha (6 years)
2. Chandra dasha (10 years)
3. Bhama dasha (7 years)
4. Rahu dasha (18 years)
5. Budha dasha (18 years)
6. Guru dasha (16 years)
7. Shani dasha (19 years)
8. Rahu dasha (17 years)
9. Ketu dasha (7 years)
10. Shukra Mahadasha (20 years)

In my opinion, the period of Mahadasha should synchronize with the psycho-physical growth of persons. The old system informs us that the period of Shukra comes at the end. This is rationally untenable.

I will suggest the following change in keeping with the psycho-physical growth of human beings.

1. Surya dasha
2. Chandra dasha
3. Bhauma dasha
4. Shukra dasha
5. Budha dasha
6. Guru dasha
7. Shani dasha
8. Rahu dasha
9. Ketu dasha

Surya being the very life must come first. Chandra denotes mind. Mental growth comes next. Mangal denotes strength. It remains from the age of 17 to 23 years. This is the period when bodily and mental strength is at its highest. Then there should be the period of Shukra. It is the period of married life. Then should come the period of Budha which stands for practical thinking. Then should come the period of Guru which stands for spiritual tendency.

Then should come the period of Rahu and Ketu should follow thereafter.

Second modification should be that the period of Surya should start right from the date of birth. Thus, calculation of periods shall be made from the Surya period in every chart uniformly and the full period of Surya viz. six years shall be counted. The subsequent period of Chandra, Mangal (Bhauma), Sukra, Budha, Guru, Shani, Rahu and Ketu as given in the system shall be counted. This will give a logical and rational view of the whole system and shall be in tune with the psycho-physical growth of human beings as narrated by modern psychology.

Our traditional system must have its own arguments. Due respect to the old system has to be given. But as Shankara has stated, logic must be always respected. If the scriptures say that fire does not burn, we should not accept this statement blindly. Kalidas a too has stated that what is old is not always good and what is new is not always bad. A happy harmony between the old and the new points of view has to be made for progress.

An objection may be made that if Surya Dasha is accepted uniformly as the starting point in every horoscope, there should be uniformity in the results. But this objection is not proper as the positions of other planets too has to be given due importance while making any judgement about the future.

Moreover, even in the traditional system, this flaw can be detected. Every moment lakhs of persons are taking birth in the world. But their destinies are different. The factors like parentage, country, time, society, etc., too must be given due consideration while making any prediction. Predictions are mere generalities. The distinguishing factor is the intuition of the predictor.

Hence the new suggested system deserves an acceptance on logical grounds.

If an astrologer predicts anything to a person, it is his knowledge of astrology plus his intuition that impels him to do so. Cheiro had predicted to Rasputin that he would be murdered and his body shall be thrown in the river Volga, he did so through the above mentioned factors.

5

THREE GUNAS

Indian philosophy accepts that the entire nature and virtually everything in this world, is constituted by three Gunas viz. Satva, Rajas and Tamasa. This theory has been accepted even by the *Bhagavad Gita— tribirguna may air bhavairebhih sarvamidam jagat*—this world is constituted by three Gunas-declares the *Bhagavad Gita* (VII-13). *Gunapravriddha vishaya-pravalah*— all subjects are driven by three Gunas repeats the Geeta (XV-2) Satva, Rajas, Tamasa—these Gunas are the constituents of nature. (VIV-5)

Although this theory of three Gunas has been widely accepted by Indian philosophy, its most systematic exposition is found in the Samakhya system. Kapila is supposed to be its first systematizer. His name has been mentioned very significantly in the Geeta. Lord Krishna declares: 'Of the great sages, I am Kapila'. The *Bhagavata Purana* describes him as a partial incarnation of Vishnu.

According to the Samakhya, the two basic substances are Purusha and Prakriti. The entire creation emanates from Prakriti (matter) which is ever changing. This Prakriti is constituted by three Gunas— Satva, Rajas and Tamas.

Everything that we find in the world contains all these three Gunas. The three Gunas occur in various relative intensities and they thus determine the properties of things.

These three Gunas are the bundles of energies, essentially distinct from each other and in a way antagonistic to each other, but can never be separated. These Gunas are the material cause of the psychic and physical universe and their characteristics are known from their products.

The presence of these three Gunas in everything can be proved from the examples in our daily life.

Three Gunas and the Planets

The nine planets too can be understood in the light of the three Gunas. Every planet has three constituents viz. Satva, Rajas, and Tamas. These states can be judged from the states of debilation, exaltation and association. Moreover, all planets are not alike in nature. There are planets in which Satva dominates. Then there are planets in which Rajas dominates. There are also planets in which Tamas dominates. The dominating element and its degree determines nature of planets. Of course, the fact remains that every planet contains all the three elements, i.e., Gunas because by nature every planet is constituted by three Gunas.

On the basis of dominance of Satva, Rajas or Tamas elements, we can say which planets are dominated by which elements.

Planets with Dominance of Satvika Elements

Guru, Chandra

Planets with Dominance of Rajasika Elements

The following planets are Rajasika as rajas dominates in them: Surya, Budha, Shukra, Mangal

Planets with Dominance of Tamasika Elements

The following planets are Tamasika as Tamas dominates in them:

Shani, Rahu and Ketu.

Similarly, Vakri (retrograde) planets too are Tamasika. If a mild planet like Guru or Budha becomes retrograde, it becomes Tamasika for the time being, thus it becomes powerful and acts with double energy.

The ownership of the houses like sixth, eighth and twelfth are Tamasika. A planet associated with the planets of these houses too assumes Tamasika colour.

To give some examples, Shani in Mesha being debilated will give Tamasika results. But if Shani is in Tula, it will give Satvika results. If Guru owns sixth house, it will give Tamasika results. If Chandra though owner of tenth house is associated with the lord of sixth house, it will give Tamasika results. However, it should not be taken too rigidly.

Nature of Three Gunas

Before mentioning the proofs for the universal presence of these Gunas, it will be better to have acquaintence with the nature of these Gunas.

Satva

It is light *(laghu)*, manifesting *(prakashaka)* and bliss or enjoyment *(Ishta)*. Where this Guna is present, these qualities too are present. A light thing goes upward, for example, the flames of fire go upward. This upward movement becomes possible due to Satva. Knowledge manifests an object. This is because of Satva. The feelings of joy, happiness, satisfaction, etc. appear in mind because of Satva.

Rajas

It is fickle and makes an object move. Moving section is possible only because of it. Air blows, mind moves, senses move towards their objects only because of it. Satva and Tamas both are inactive by nature. Both become active only because of Rajas. Rajas generates pain. Hence when Rajas dominates, one does become active, but the result is only pain.

Tamas

It is heavy (guru) and obstructing. It is contradictory to Satva. It obstructs the movement of Rajas. If Tamas will not obstruct Rajas will be all the while moving. It generates ignorance and delusion. It is responsible for darkness and sloth of intelligence. It creates the states of laziness, sleep, sloth.

Colours have been given to there Gunas. Satva is white and shining; Rajas is red; and Tamas is dark and black.

Interrelation Between the Three Gunas

Although the three Gunas differ in nature and are sometimes contradictory, they always act conjointly. They are never separate. For example, oil, wick and fire are divergent in character, but they combine to light an earthen lamp. A constant fight for supremacy, however, goes on in the realm of Gunas. Satva tries to subdue Rajas and Tamas; Rajas tries to subdue Satva and Tamas and Tamas tries to subdue Satva and Rajas.

Proofs for the Three Gunas

The Samkhya system believes that the entire universe has sprung from Prakriti. The world has evolved out of Prakriti, which is constituted by three Gunas viz. Satva, Rajas and Tamas. Hence, everything that we find in creation contains all these constituents. And there is proof for this fact.

If we just look at anything in the world, we find in it the presence of all the three Gunas. For example, there are mangoes in a tree. The boys try to have them in their own ways. They are pleased at the sight of the mangoes. Their pleasure becomes all the more intense when they procure them by climbing the tree. This is because of the Satva present in the mangoes. But the owner of the tree feels displeased with this. This is because of the Tamas present in them. And spectators who just stand by the side remain indifferent. This is because of the Tamas present in them.

A musical melody pleases a lover of music; but it displeases a patient and others just remain indifferent. A beautiful lady pleases her husband, displeases her rivals, and produces delusion in the spectators. Thus, it is apparent that Satva, Rajas and Tamas constitute Prakriti from which everything has evolved. Prakriti is ever changing.

Hence, we have to accept that Satva, Rajas and Tamas are present in every being including planets. This fact will enable us to understand the triple aspects of a planet.

Even a Mahadasha of a planet is bound to give three aspects of period. If we examine it minutely.

6

LAGNA RASHI

Lagna Rashi has supreme significance. There are twelve Rashis, according to Indian astrology viz. Mesha, Vrishabha, Mithuna, Karka, Simha, Kanya, Tula, Vrishchik, Dhanu, Makara, Kumbha and Meena. Lagna must fall under any one of these Rashis. Hence a short description of the nature of each Rashi is desirable.

Mesha

Mangal is the lord of this Rashi. He has medium size, whitish colour. His temperament is hot. He is courageous and commanding and cannot brook any subordination. He is obstinate and insists on his way. He is outspoken. He is the lord of land.

Hence, Mesha signifies an outspoken, dashing, to some extent hasty nature. It also signifies a love for journey, disdain for remaining at one place for a long time, love for landed property, pursuit of militant activities, insubordination, and utmost importance to self-respect.

A person ruled by this sign is expected to have these qualities to a lesser or greater extent. Of course, aspect of any planet may modify them to certain extent. The placing of Surya in this position indicates a strong tendency to dominate and become influential. This sign is represented by a goat, which by nature is ready to fight, if provoked.

Vrishabha

Vrishabha Rashi is owned by Venus. But it is represented by a bull. A person with this Lagna has the characteristics of Venus. He is fond of sensual pleasures, likes music and amusement, but at the same time is not willing to take things as they come to him. If he dislikes any view or thing, he is prepared to fight. Bull also signifies a tendency to work hard in a way one likes. Hence, a person under the sign is painstaking, worldly, adacious but ready to follow any point of view to a certain extent. He is, however, ready to revolt if he is cornered and is not afraid of giving a good fight.

Mithuna

A characteristic feature of this Rashi is that it always has before it both the aspects of a point of view or problem. Hence, it faces a sense of indecision at times.

But this Rashi indicates a tendency of learning, reading and writing it also indicates a sense of humour and wit. It indicates an introvert tendency which gives it a thinker's habit. It also indicates a spirit of adjustment. It also indicates a practical, commercial bent of mind.

Due to a rational attitude, this Rashi bestows an arguing and mentally alive habit.

Karka

This Rashi bestows white colour to a person. This Rashi being Chandrama's Rashi, beauty is indicated. Moon is also known for its fancies, hence a fanciful nature is indicated. Imagination is needed even for creative purpose. Hence a poetic tendency too is indicated. It also shows fondness for journey.

A sense of doing justice to one and all is also evident.

It bestows an agile mind and therefore it gives good intelligence and sense of grasping things.

By nature, this Rashi indicates a transparent tendency. A person having this Rashi cannot hide anything. Be it indignation, hatred, love and affection—everything is apparent.

A person of this Rashi chooses a path of devotion, if it comes to an attainment of God. A sense of genuine devotion marks his prayer. A sense of sincerity is the hallmark of this Rashi.

This Rashi denotes an unsteady nature too.

Simha

A strong and influential personality is indicated by this sign, because lion happens to be the king of forest. The upper part of the body is comparatively heavier than the lower part of the body. Personality is marked by fearlessness, dominating tendency, ambitiousness, zestfulness and uncompromising attitude. This sign makes a person liberal hearted and helpful to the needy. A person of this sign can get easy success in the domain of politics.

Kanya

This sign makes a person intelligent and practical. He likes business rather than service. He can make a good accountant, salesman, bank officer, journalist, planner, master of computer science, etc.

A person ruled by this sign is very eager to earn money. To become a rich person is his fad.

Being practical, a person of this sign tries to make adjustments everywhere and thereto can pull on with any person. He is tolerant and a hard worker. He is tactful and methodical.

Tula

This Rashi symbolizes a sense of balance in thought and demeanour. It also denotes a love for justice and fair play. As the owner of this Rashi happens to be Shukra, this Rashi makes a person a lover of good fashionable dresses and luxuries. A love for art and light literature too is indicated. This Rashi being movable indicates a love for journey and change.

Being balanced, this Rashi cannot tolerate any undue influence and can revolt, if pressed too much.

Owners of this Rashi can do well in the field of art, designing, law, business of artistic items, salesmanship, film acting and any work which attracts the ladies.

Vrishchik

This Rashi indicates a person who is obstinate, perseverant and dashing. A person of this Rashi is a cruel enemy. He feels pleasure in hurting the sentiments of others. He speaks piercing words at times. He feels pleasure in cutting ungenerous jokes at the cost of others.

A person of this Rashi does not like to make unnecessary journey. He prefers to stay home and does not like the discomforts of making tours as far as possible.

Dhanu

This Rashi stands for intelligence, ambition, love for truthfulness and liberalness of heart and mind. A love for spirituality is also indicated as the lord of this Rashi happens to be Guru. A religious life and love for God marks the life of a person of this Rashi. A person of this Rashi can fly into anger on a legitimate ground, but he becomes pacified soon. As Guru also rules law, this Rashi gives a good knowledge of law to a person interested in it. If this Rashi is powerful, success in legal work too is indicated.

Makara

Lord of this Rashi is Shani. Hence this Rashi gives a tendency of keeping patience and painstakingness. It also indicates faithfulness and a sense of discipline. A person of this Rashi does not believe in making too many friends. He loves to lead a lonely and peaceful life. A person of this Rashi can become popular even in the domain of politics and can meet the opponent's challenges very patiently.

A person of this Rashi can be a good officer in any public institutions. He can prosper in business concerned with oil or machinery.

Kumbha

The lord of this Rashi is Shani. By nature this Rashi is secretive. A person of this Rashi does not believe in talking much. He thinks it proper not to reveal all his secrets. He may become a lover of meditation. He restricts his company and speaks only after due thinking. As he is thoughtful; he cannot change his attitude easily and sticks to his thinking.

A person of this Rashi is capable of reaching top position so far as the spiritual pursuit is concerned.

This does not give any liking for useless journey. It indicates a capacity of an inner growth in a person.

Meena

This Rashi indicates indecisive tendency. But the nature is noble and soft. The person of this Rashi can easily make adjustments in any type of situation. Liberalness marks the attitude of the person of this Rashi. Religious tendency too is present.

7
PLANETS

Planets are the most important part of astrology. Although they have a symbolic character, their physical being too has much importance. Most of the people consider them to be concrete beings. They are pleased; they are displeased; they like to be worshipped; they give boon; they give curse.

In Indian astrology they have been given certain peculiar descriptions. Indian mind has a distinctive feature. It accepts two forms: one subtle and the other concrete. Thus, we have mother Ganga. She runs from the Himalayas to plains and reaches Calcutta. But this is only her concrete form. Behind this concrete form stands the subtle form of Ganga which can be invoked anywhere and which comes forward to the rescue of a devotee at latter's intense request. Rivers, mountains, trees and deities all have these two aspects, one local and the other universal. Thus Shiva is in the temple at Varanasi and yet He is omnipresent and can be invoked anywhere.

Even the Ragas and Raginis have been given certain forms, which are objective and have been allotted certain universal aspects which can be experienced by some talented persons, alone.

Grahas too have this dual aspect.

Indian astrology accepts the existence of nine planets, viz. Surya, Chandra, Mangal, Budha, Shukra, Guru, Shani, Rahu and Ketu.

Let us try to understand them in the way they have been accepted and understood.

We shall start from Surya, because it is the most important planet. Linked with these planets are the twelve Rashis too. Their description has already been given.

Surya

Surya is the key planet in astrology. Its unique features are stated below in short:

Colour		Red or copper
Age		About 50 years
Appearance		Beautiful and impressive
Sex		Male
Caste		Kshatriya
Parts of body ruled by it		Head and face
Status		King
Period of rise of fortune		22 to 24 years of age
Signification	:	Soul, Father, Nature, Prosperity, Health, Prowess
II. **Relation with other Planets**		
Friendly planets	:	Chandra, Mangal, Guru and Ketu
Enemical planets	:	Shani, Shukra, Rahu
Neutral	:	Budha
III. Exalted Rashi	:	Mesha
Rashi of debilation	:	Tula
IV. Best position	:	Mesha
Medium position	:	Mithuna, Karka, Kanya, Dhanu, Meena
Good	:	Simha
Average	:	Vrishabha, Makar, Vrishchika, Kumbha
Bad	:	Tula
V. Position in Houses (Bhavas)		
Good	:	3, 6, 10 and 11
VI. Vocations indicated	:	Political career, Administration, military career Good Surya gives commanding position in every profession.

Chandra

Colour	:	White
Appearance	:	Beautiful
Age	:	Youth
Caste	:	Vaishya
Nature	:	Fickle
Influence on the parts of body	:	From throat to heart
Period of rise	:	24 to 25
Significator	:	Mind, intelligence, mother, riches, happiness, progress

II. Relation with other planets:

Friendly	:	Surya, Budha
Even	:	Mangal, Guru, Shukra, Shani, Rahu, Ketu

No enemy

III. Exalted in Vrishabha,

Debilated in Vrishchika

IV. Houses

Rules 4th house

Good house positions	:	1, 3, 6, 7, 10, 11
V. Nature	:	Satvika, modest, intelligent, calm, lover of fancy and imagination, fond of movement and travelling, sensitive.
VI. Temperament	:	Lover of art, music, literature, poetry, acting

Bhauma or Mangal

It is called god of war. That is why it is known as Angaraka too

Colour	:	Red
Age	:	Young
Sex	:	Male
Appearance	:	Thin-bodied
Caste	:	Kshatriya

Position	: Commander-in-chief of army.
Influence on parts of body	: Stomach and back.
Period of rise	: From 28 to 32
Subjects covered	: Prowess, activeness, land, brother

II. Relation with other planets :

Friendly	: Surya, Chandra, Guru
Even	: Shukra and Shani

III.	Exaltation	: Makara
	Debilation	: Karka
	Own Rashis	: Mesha and Vrishchika
IV.	Best when in Makara	
	Good when in Mesha	
	Even	: Simha, Kanya, Vrishchika, Dhanu, Meena, Vrishabha, Mithun
V.	House positions	
	Good houses	: 3, 6, 11
VI.	Nature	: Courageous, aggressive, Leader
VII.	Occupations ruled by it	: Military, spying, pleader, medical, matters concerning land and houses

Shukra

It represents worldly pleasures and attitudes.

Colour	: White
Age	: Adolescent
Appearance	: Attractive
Nature	: Soft
Caste	: Brahmin
Position	: Confident
Hobbies	: Music, play, art
Period of rise in life	: From 25 to 28
Occupations	: Literature, artist, fine arts

II. Relation with other planets :

Friendly	:	Budha, Shani, Rahu
Even	:	Mangal, Guru, and Ketu

III. Exaltation	:	Meena
Debilation	:	Kanya

Best when in Meena

Good when in Vrishabha, Tula

Average when in Mithuna, Karka, Dhanu, Makara, Kumbha

IV. House position

Good	:	1, 2, 3, 4, 9, 11, 12
V. Occupations		Artist, musician, actor, decorator, jeweller, cosmetic, work, photographer, bar, restaurant, etc.

Budha

Colour	:	Green
Age	:	Adolescent
Appearance	:	Happy
Sex	:	Neutral
Caste	:	Shudra
Status	:	Prince
Aptitude	:	Accountancy
Period of rise	:	From 32 to 36 years of age
Subjects concerned	:	Learning, discrimination, adaptibility

II. Relation with other planets:

Friendly	:	Surya, Shukra,
Even	:	Other planets
III. Exaltation	:	Kanya Rashi
Debilation	:	Meena Rashi

IV. Best	:	Kanya Rashi
Good	:	Mithuna and Tula
V. House positions :		
Good	:	2, 4, 6, 8, 10, 11
VI. Temperament	:	Budha denotes good power of conversation, writing, accountancy, legal matters, journalism, management, commercial intelligence, book-publication, speaking, etc. Apart from these professions, Budha can give proficiency in any other work governed by a planet associated with Budha.

Practical point of view is indicated by Budha.

Guru

Colour	:	Yellow
Age	:	Old age
Appearance	:	Fat
Sex	:	Male
Nature	:	Soft
Caste	:	Brahmin
Period of rise	:	16 to 22 years of age
Significant for	:	spirituality, progeny and happiness.
II. Relation with other planets:		
Friendly	:	Surya, Chandra, Mangal, Ketu
III. Exaltation	:	Karka
Debilation in Makara		
IV. House positions		
Good	:	2, 5, 7, 9, 11
V. Temperament	:	Virtuous, good adviser

VI. Professions	:	Preacher, teacher, social reformer, preceptor, judge, philosopher, astrologer

Shani

Colour	:	Black
Age	:	Old
Appearance	:	Indolent
Sex	:	Neutral
Size	:	Tall
Position	:	Servant
Parts of body governed	:	Knee
Aptitude	:	Philosophy, law, diplomacy
Period of rise	:	36 years of age onwards
Subjects considered	:	Age, unhappiness
II. Relation with other planets:		
Friendly	:	Budha, Shukra, Rahu
III. Exaltation	:	Tula
Debilation	:	Mesha
Best	:	Tula,
Good	:	Makara and Kumbha
IV. House position	:	Good in 3, 6, 11
V. Profession	:	Law, philosophy, diplomacy, foreign land and language, engineering, renunciation, preacher, printing press, oil, iron, psychology, photography, popularity

Rahu

Colour	:	Blue
Age	:	Very Old
Appearance	:	Unclean
Sex	:	Female
Size	:	Tall

Caste	:	Outcaste
Aptitude	:	Esotoric knowledge, occult
Period of rise	:	From 42 years of age onwards
Subjects considered	:	Ancestors

II. Relation with other planets:

Friendly	:	Budha, Shukra, Shani
Neutral	:	Guru, Ketu
Exaltation	:	Mithuna
Debilation	:	Dhanu
Best Rashi	:	Mithuna
Good Rashis	:	Kanya, Simha, Vrishchika, Meena

III. House position :

Best	:	3, 6, 10, 11

IV. Profession	:	Foreign journey, Tantrik, Diplomacy, opportunism espionage

Ketu

Colour	:	Smokey
Age	:	Very old
Appearance	:	Unclean
Sex	:	Female
Size	:	Puny
Caste	:	Outcaste
Parts of body governed	:	Skin and nerves
Period of rise	:	From 46 years onwards
Aptitude	:	Tantras-mantra, esotoric

II. Relation with other planets:

Friendly	:	Budha, Surya, Shani, Guru
Exaltation	:	Dhanu
Debilation	:	Mithuna
		Generally Rahu and Ketu give the result of the planet or planets, and

		the Rashi or Rashis with which they become associated.
III. House position	:	Good in 3, 6, 10 and 11
IV. Profession	:	It makes a person a spy, vendor of medicines, lover of antiquated things, Yogi, inventer, mystic, deep thinker.

8

THE GRAHAS (PLANETS)

In Indian thought symbolism dominates. If Rama, Krishna, Shiva and other gods are symbols of the Brahman or the supreme Reality, even Grahas are symbols. In *Ramayana,* Rama and Ravana are the symbols of the Good and the Evil respectively. Similarly, Krishna and Kamsa are the symbols of the Good and the Evil respectively. Sometimes the symbolism is so hidden in a story, which is meant for the lay man, that one misses it at the first sight. That is why the foreigners think that India accepts a plurality of gods, while the basic Indian thought says that one Real alone manifests itself in various names and forms out of Lila or divine play.

Persons have different and divergent likings and aptitudes. They consider the Real in the light of these tendencies and likings. In whatever form they worship the Real, all their worships go to the Real just as all the rivers merge in the ocean.

Ruchinam vaichitryad riju-kutila nana pathajusham
nrinameko gamya tavamasi payasamarnave iva.

Not only gods like Ganesha, Lakshmi, Sarasvati, but even planets like Surya, Chandra, Mangal, Budha, Shukra, Guru, Rahu and Ketu are just symbols. A person is substantially the Virat Purusha. Surya is present in his head and mouth; Chandrama is present is his breast and neck; Mangal is present in his stomach and back; Budha is present in his hands and feet; Guru is present in his waist and thighs; Shukra is present in his sexual organs; Shani is present in the knees.

Human body houses different Rashis. Mesha is present in the head; Vrishabha Rashi is present in the mouth; Mithuna Rashi is present in the arms; Karka Rashi is present in the heart; Simha

Rashi is present in the stomach; Kanya Rashi is present in the waist; Tula Rashi is present in the urinary organs; Vrishchika Rashi is present in the sexual organs; Dhanu Rashi is present in the thighs; Makara Rashi is present in the knees; Kumbha Rashi is present in the portion below the knees; Meena Rashi is present in the feet.

Even the houses of a chart have been given symbolic meanings. Thus the Ist house (lagna) represents head; 2nd house represents mouth; 3rd house represents the arms; 4th house represents heart; 5th house represents stomach; 6th house represents waist; 7th house represents Vasti; 8th house represents sexual organs; 9th house represents *uru* (thighs); 10th house represents *janu* (knee); 11th house represents *jangha* and 12th house represents the feet.

Every horoscope reflects the psycho-physical nature of a person. The planets can be understood yet from another angle. A person is ruled by certain dominant sentiments *(rasa)* like love, anger, conflict, erotic feelings, etc. The various planets symbolize various sentiments.

Surya	Soul-power or *Atmic* power
Chandra	Mental attitude
Mangal	Courage
Budha	Practical intelligence
Guru	Spiritual tendency
Shukra	Carnal desires and physical comfort
Shani	Ascetic tendency and loneliness.
Rahu	Represents the tendency of the Rashi it occupies. But it also denotes some destructive leanings.
Ketu	Represents the tendency of the Rashi it occupies. But it also represents occult tendencies.

Thus we find that the whole scheme of the planets and chart contains some deeper meaning, which may not be grasped by a layman.

PART II

PLANETS IN DIFFERENT HOUSES AND THEIR INFLUENCE

9

MESHA LAGNA

There are twelve houses. If a planet is present in a house it gives certain results. Of course these results contain only possibilities; but astrology is based on possibilities alone.

Now, let us try to see the result of a planet in the first house which is Mesha.

We shall start from Surya:

Surya's Position in Mesha Lagna

House	Effects
(I)	Good personality, hot temperament, good education, commanding position, good children.
(II)	Education with obstruction, gains from children.
(III)	Very active, intelligent, power of speech, influential brothers, courageous.
(IV)	Some problems of domestic life, prestige in the work, liveliness, education with some hindrance.
(V)	Good education and popularity, accidental opportunities giving rise in life, lucky children, farsightedness.
(VI)	Destruction of enemies and obstacles, worries from enemies.
(VII)	Some problems in marriages, marriage may be delayed, maladjustment with wife.
(VIII)	Interest in occult sciences, harsh speech, some worries in life.
(IX)	High education, gets popularity, religious mindedness, satisfaction from progeny, unexpected gains and opportunities of rise.

(X) Top position in occupation, favoured by the superior officers or influential persons.

(XI) Gain from children, earning through intelligence and cooperation from political leaders and influential persons and officers.

(XII) Weak eyesight, weak intelligence, some problems from progeny, good contact with outsiders, destruction of enemies and opposition.

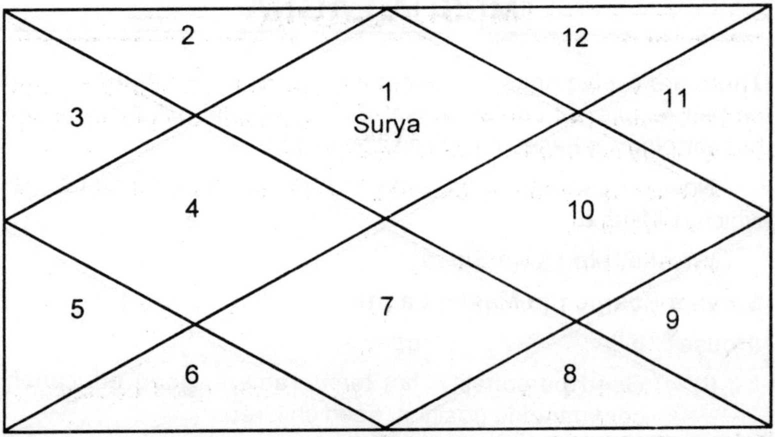

Chandrama's Position in Mesha Lagna:

House Effects

(I) Happiness and pleasure, gets mother's blessings and happiness, likely to have landed property, beautiful face, beautiful and loving wife.

(II) Wealthy, owner of landed property, favoured by mother, religious temperament.

(III) Pleasure of brothers and sisters, gets fame, has faith in God, gets brother's help and cooperation in building career.

(IV) Good hearted, contented, loved by mother, has fondness for domestic happiness.

(V) Intelligent, educated, many progenies, sweet-tongued, good thinker, respecter of mother.

(VI) Hindrances in getting mother's happiness, spend-thrift, worried by enemies, spends money on good items.

(VII) Beautiful wife, gets mother's help, gets land and housing facilities, skilful in handling family matters.

(VIII) Weak motherly love, possibility of loss in immovable property, dissatisfaction of heart.

(IX) Fortunate mother, facilities of landed property, follower of religion, helpful brothers, and sisters, virtuous life.

(X) Loved by mother, gets motherly affection, possibility of gaining landed property, happy domestic life, peace and contentment.

(XI) Fluctuating income, gains of landed property, good income due to mother's blessings, happiness from progeny, good education, favoured by good luck.

(XII) Expenditure on luxuries, away from the place of birth, possibility of settling out of native city or nation, has to confront hindrances from enemies, mental discomfort, unhelpful family.

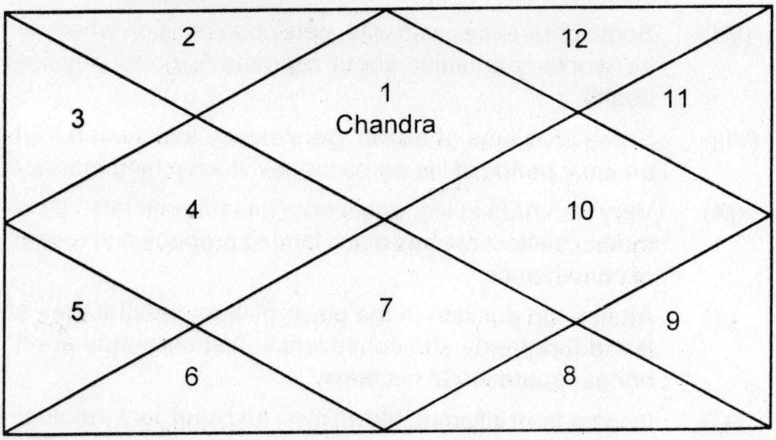

Mangal's Position in Mesha Lagna

House	Effects
(I)	Strong build, mother's happiness lacking, good longevity, liable to some kind of operation, short height, obstinate, uncompromising when it comes to principles, can shine in sports, can bear hardship with courage.
(II)	Earns livelihood through hard work, first child may abort, outspoken, something lacking in family life.
(III)	Quite energetic, some difference of opinion with brothers and sisters, gets importance in the domain of service or business, overcomes enemies, development of career from the age of twenty-eight.
(IV)	Discontented on the home front, lack of harmony with wife, had to struggle in life.
(V)	Outspoken, good longevity, ambitious and dashing.
(VI)	Overcomes enemies and obstructions, gets some health problems right from birth, may be operated, brave, spends lavishly when money comes.
(VII)	Some differences with wife, gets good position wherever he works, particular about reputation, good physical health.
(VIII)	Some problems of health, gets elderly looks even from an early period of life earns money in a dashing manner.
(IX)	Very fortunate in life, gains from distant relations, lacks mother's affection, has much landed property and means of conveyance.
(X)	Attains top position in the place of work, advantages of landed property and conveyance, first child may abort, brings reputation to his family.
(XI)	Income from inflammable articles, and land, lucky mother, can go out of way to earn money.

(XII) Some problem of health at least in the early childhood, difference of opinion with brothers, defeats his enemies, some problems concerning wife.

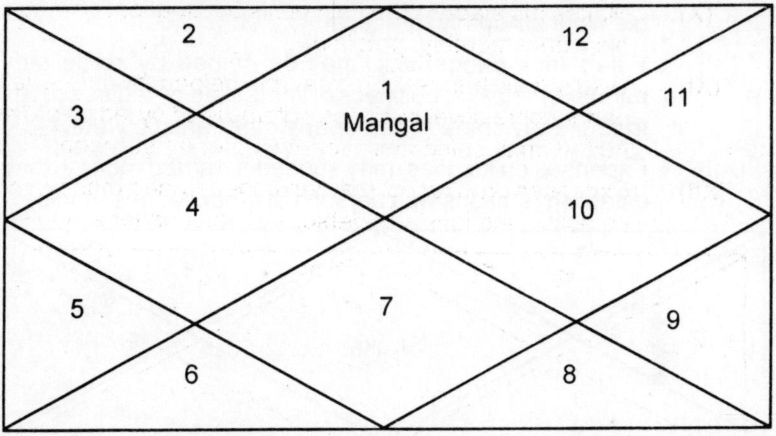

Shukra in Mesha Lagna

House	Effects
(I)	Handsome personality, beautiful wife, sense of aesthetics, good health and prosperity.
(II)	Good amount of wealth, happy family life, lucky wife, fond of luxuries.
(III)	Good relations with brothers and sisters, happy worldly wife.
(IV)	Beautiful and graceful wife, property and means of conveyance, smoothness in work, peaceful family life.
(V)	Money earned through intellectual work, may have first issue a daughter, may have connection with some artistic work, fond of music and melodies.
(VI)	Some problems from wife and family worries diplomatic temperament.
(VII)	Beautiful wife and wealthy father-in-law, gives good looks to a person.
(VIII)	Good and happy family life, gains from artistic and absorbing work, may get money from the side of father-in-law.

(IX) Thrives due to the good luck of wife, has a material outlook, respectable and happy.

(X) Makes his place in the field of his occupation, carries on his work smoothly, practical.

(XI) Wife's luck brings luck, may be helped by some lady partner or relative, business of items liked by ladies proves fruitful, may shine in film or any other artistic work.

(XII) Expenses on luxuries, may squander earned money, may establish relations with persons of other nations, and sex.

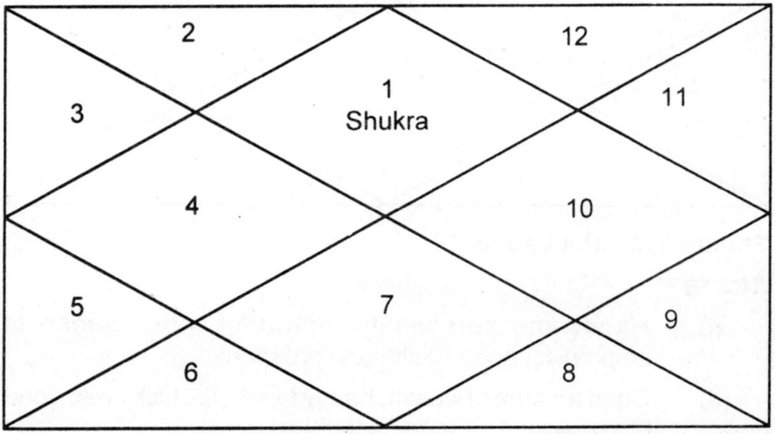

Position of Budha in Mesha Lagna

House Effects

(I) Great mental and practical power, can solve problems in a prudent manner, practical and wise wife.

(II) Money earning through business, some lack of harmony with brothers, creates some disatisfaction in the family environment.

(III) Acts with intelligence and foresight. Makes a person active all the while.

(IV) Help from brothers and one's own efforts, some anxieties from enemies or obstacles.

(V) Smart talker, not very friendly progeny, practical thinking, good relations with brothers and sisters, earns reputation through conversational skill.

(VI) Uncordial relations with brothers, obstruction in the fulfilment of efforts.

(VII) Gets help from brothers and sisters, fulfilment of the efforts made for achieving any objective.

(VIII) Undesirable relations with brothers, pursuit of occult powers, faces difficulties with courage and intelligence.

(IX) Fame and success, no real interest in religious work, a thorough worldly objective in life. May succeed in commercial work.

(X) Excellent help from brothers and sisters. Earns success through intelligent planning in life, good relations with mother.

(XI) Very helpful and influential brothers, gets success in whatever one may try, no enemy can harm, good command over speech.

(XII) A lack of brothers or strife with brothers and sisters, restless due to enemies, dependence on others in financial matters.

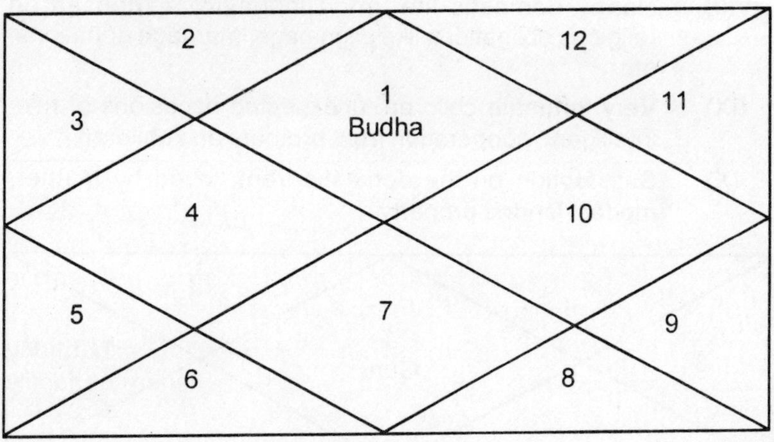

Guru's Position in Mesha Lagna

House	Effects
(I)	Handsome, fortunate and respected by people. Has more sons as compared to daughters, educated, noble-minded.
(II)	Fortunate, tactfully handles enemies and obstacles, smooth-sailing in service or occupation, religious-mindedness.
(III)	Very fortunate, good cooperation from brothers, famous, earning through straight-forward means.
(IV)	Smooth working in the occupation, some discontent from the domestic scene.
(V)	Very fortunate, educated, religious temperament, impressive speech power, fortunate children.
(VI)	Struggle in life, rise after 16 years of age, expenditure on reasonable items.
(VII)	Good health, slow but steady income, respected by people, laborious.
(VIII)	Happy domestic life, good longevity, expenses on religious obligations like pilgrimage, marriage donations, etc.
(IX)	Very fortunate children, unexpected occasions of rise, intelligent, cooperation from brothers and children.
(X)	Satisfaction on the domestic front, loved by mother, modest landed property.

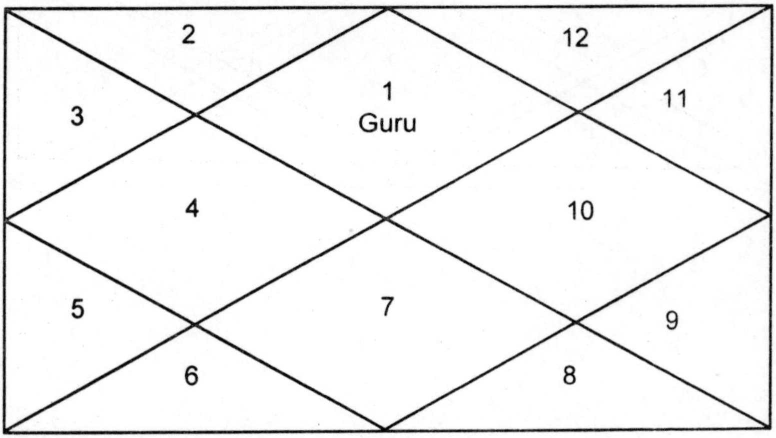

(XI) Industrious, steady income through legitimate means, educated, male children.

(XII) Spiritual tendency, happy family life, spends on proper occasions, struggle for rise, has almost no enemies.

Shani's Position in Mesha Lagna

House	Effects
(I)	Not handsome laborious, some type of worry, laziness, lack of harmony so far as the wife is concerned, miserly habits.
(II)	Good monetary gains, unpalatable relations with mother, some problems on domestic front.
(III)	Very active and laborious, makes progress by dint of labour, some dissatisfaction from progeny.
(IV)	Unsmooth conditions in the place of occupation, some problems regarding health, overpowers one's enemies and obstacles, unsatisfactory home conditions.
(V)	Profit from father, deficient conjugal relationship, money earning through self-effort, some difference of opinion with children.
(VI)	Victory over enemies, some lack of paternal affection, spends money prudently.
(VII)	Gains from father, top money earning after the age of 36 years, some problems from home, makes rise after a successful struggle.
(VIII)	Good longevity, may gain from foreign nations, interest in occult science, worries from children.
(IX)	Money earning through struggles, laborious by nature, victorious.
(X)	Successful industrialist or political leader, not favoured by the mother, spends money wisely.
(XI)	Very good money-earner, gets parental advantages, some problems concerning health.

(XII) Spends recklessly, interest in meditation or philosophic and yogic methods.

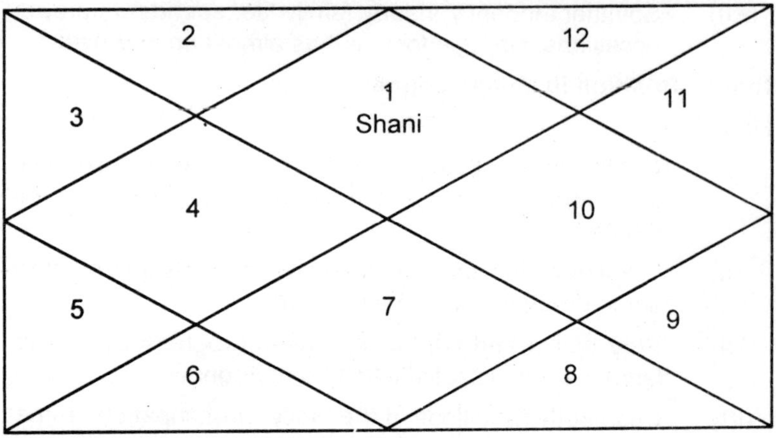

Rahu's Position in Mesha Lagna

House	Effects
(I)	Some bodily troubles, capable of taking great risks, acts in a secret manner, may be required to undergo some medical operation, some scar on the face possible.
(II)	Some monetary loss indicated, some disruption of family is also likely, rise after 42 years of age.
(III)	Diplomat, capable of undertaking dubious acts too for one's worldly progress, shrewd.
(IV)	Domestic dissatisfaction, lacks motherly protection, lacks mental peace.
(V)	May have difficulties in education, may have some dissatisfaction from children, first born child may face abortion or death, rash speech.
(VI)	Scores over enemies, some undesirable condition in place of work.
(VII)	Worries concerning wife, unfruitful business partnership.
(VIII)	Some abdominal trouble possible, unhappy family life, may have interest in devilish acts.
(IX)	Severe struggle for success, scheming tendency, does not care for moral ways.

(X) Worries concerning father, struggle in the domain of occupation, may not be respected by others, but may get success through cleverness.

(XI) Abundance of money, may get success through fair or foul means.

(XII) Huge expenditure, extremely brave and courageous, can get the desired object through any means.

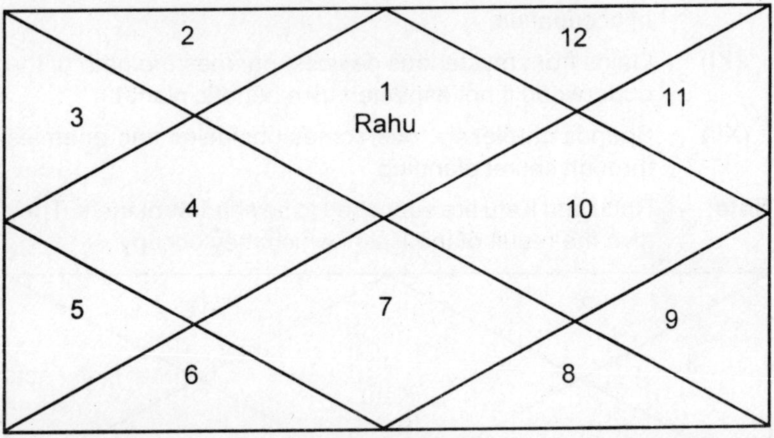

Ketu's Position in Mesha Lagna

House	Effects
(I)	Some bodily defect possible, courageous, cannot accept subordination, internal worry.
(II)	May have occasionally some monetary losses, some dissatisfaction from family possible.
(III)	Great internal strength, disharmony with brothers, acts silently but boldly, great patience.
(IV)	Separation from mother possible, builds up landed property through planned labour, some domestic problems possible.
(V)	Dissatisfaction from children, secretive tendency, does not divulge one's plans to any one.
(VI)	Defeats enemies through planning, overcomes hindrances through mental courage and thinking.

(VII) Some problems from wife possible, works secretly to achieve desired objective.

(VIII) Love for esotoric subjects, may like black magic, may have connection with the underworld.

(IX) Gets cooperation from secret agencies in fulfilment of objectives, progress after great patient work.

(X) Lack of father's affection or protection, worries in the place of occupation.

(XI) Gains from mysterious devices, pursues the path of the underworld if not aspected by a benefic planet.

(XII) Spends carelessly, overcomes obstacles and enemies through secret planning.

Note: Rahu and Ketu are supposed to be shadow planets. They give the result of the Rashi which they occupy.

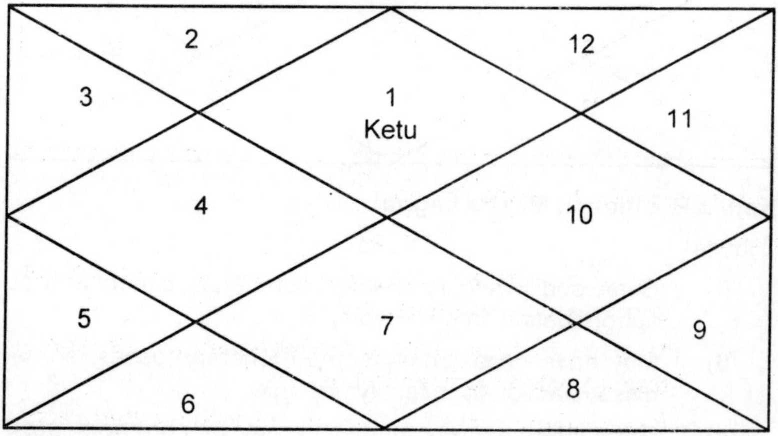

10

VRISHABHA LAGNA

Surya's Position in Vrishabha Lagna

House	Effects
(I)	Mother's affection, landed property, domestic happiness irascible nature, influential personality.
(II)	Pretty amount of wealth, advantages of property gains from mother, domestic pleasure.
(III)	Very active and dominant, helpful brothers, helped by influential persons in life.
(IV)	Happiness from property and mother, wields influence in society and place of occupation, differences in the members of family.
(V)	High education, intelligent, gain of property, hard speech, vanity.
(VI)	Separation from mother, or mother does not bestow affection, problems concerning property, overcomes opposition.
(VII)	Favoured by mother, differences with wife, pleasures of property and conveyances, hot temperament.
(VIII)	May be required to leave place of birth, may prosper in a foreign country, respect in family circle.
(IX)	Gets mother's blessings, influential, helpful brothers, help from father.
(X)	Influential, lucky due to mother, help from father.

(XI) Gains from mother, huge fortune from father, influential friends and relatives.

(XII) Luck from mother, facility of conveyance and servants, expensive habits, overcomes opposition.

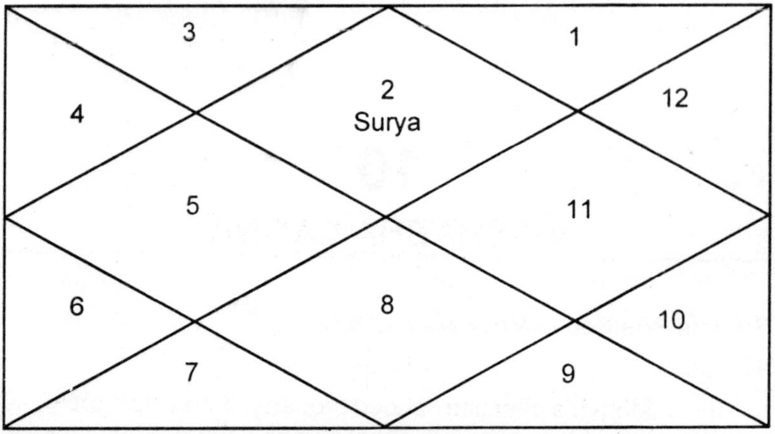

Chandrama's Position in Vrishabha Lagna

House Effects

(I) Handsome, cooperative brothers and sisters, cheerfulness, beautiful wife.

(II) Harmonious family life, accumulates money, amiable nature.

(III) Cooperative brothers and sisters, energetic, has a good friendly circle.

(IV) Good relations with brothers and sisters, landed property, domestic happiness, loves mother and motherland.

(V) Practical outlook, can adjust anywhere, good education, handsome children, witty and pleasing conversationalist.

(VI) Differences with brothers and sisters, mental tension from enemies, spends money rather carelessly.

(VII) Disharmony with wife, brothers non-cooperative, good personality, pessimistic.

(VIII) Mental tension from family, tries hard to earn money, may have foreign contacts.

(IX) Fortunate, cooperation from brothers and sisters, very active, religious-mindedness.

(X) Happy family life, happiness from mother, brothers and sisters, can keep his views secret.

(XI) Good money earning, amiable nature, pious hearted, gains from females and beautiful objects, clever, intelligent.

(XII) May live separate from brothers, spends much, can bear great patience even in midst of obstacles and adverse conditions, fearless and ready to give a fight if challenged.

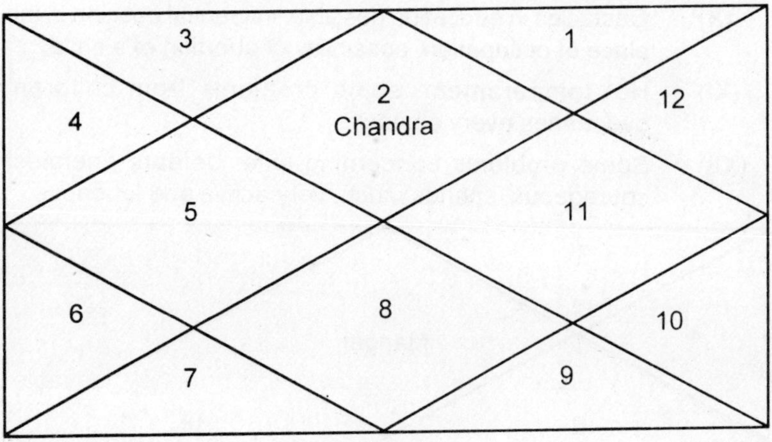

Mangal's Position in Vrishabha Lagna

House Effects

(I) Hot temperament, possibility of medical operation, landed property, some unhappiness from mother, some problems concerning wife.

(II) Some loss of property, conjugal life not very satisfactory, some problems concerning children, harsh speech possible.

(III) Some problems concerning wife, disharmony with brothers, reckless courage.

(IV) Mother's loss possible, may settle in a place distant from the place of birth, non-congenial relation with wife, dominant position in the place of occupation, gain from landed property, courageous.

(V) Obstacles in education, spends money out of proportion, earning through courage.

(VI) Faces obstruction and hindrances from enemies, but overcomes them through courage, ill health.

(VII) Hot temperament, some dissension in family, dominant position in the place of occupation.

(VIII) Family lacks harmony, very active, very courageous, gains from landed property or inflammable items.

(IX) Lucky and influential wife, fearless and courageous, rise in life after 28 years of age.

(X) Obstacles in education possible, influential position in the place of occupation, possibility of abortion of a child.

(XI) Hot temperament, some problems from children, overcomes every obstacle.

(XII) Some problems concerning wife, defeats enemies, courageous, spends much, very active and laborious.

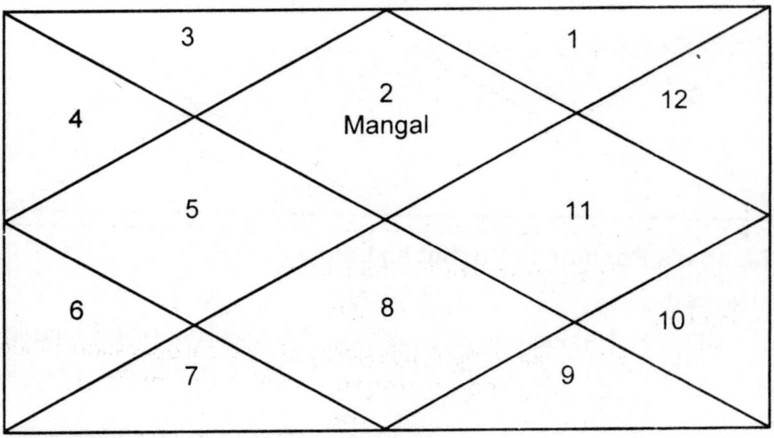

Shukra's Position in Vrishabha Lagna

House Effects

(I) Handsome personality, fond of artistic things and items of pleasure, popular amongst ladies, pretty wife, obstinate.

(II) Wealthy, happy family life, obstacles from enemies, happy conjugal life.

(III) Active, difference with brothers, lucky, materialistic, obstruction from enemies.

(IV) Happy family life, smooth working in the place of occupation, disturbed by the enemies at times.

(V) Materialistic tendency, occasional disturbance from enemies, earning from artistic activities, indecisive.

(VI) Ill health, heavy expenditure, troubled by enemies.

(VII) Handsome personality, pretty wife, fond of luxuries, thinks oneself very beautiful.

(VIII) Problem of health, happy family life, materialistic bent of mind.

(IX) Fortunate, gets success in his efforts, helpful sisters and brothers, has to struggle for progress.

(X) Happy family atmosphere, conveyance, good house, silent but popular worker.

(XI) Income from arts, company of ladies, politician, number of daughters more than that of sons, earns luxuries of life.

(XII) Spends much on luxuries, wins enemies through tactfulness, ill health, may lose money because of some female friend.

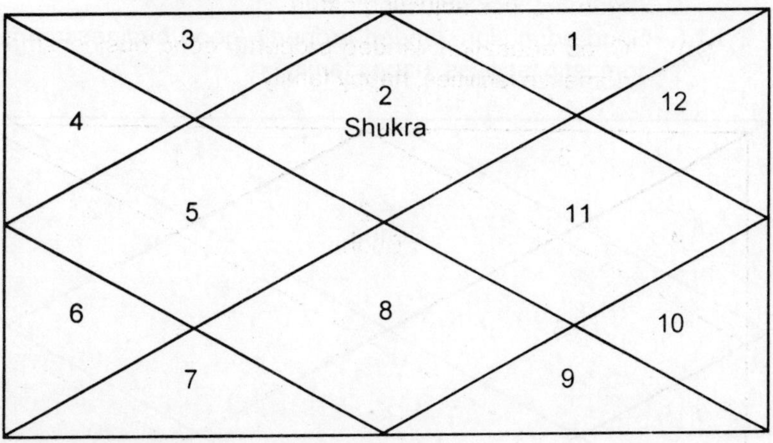

Budha's Position in Vrishbha Lagna

House	Effects
(I)	Very practical outlook, worldly-wise attitude, helpful children, good personality.
(II)	Earns money through business and preserves it, good family environment, sees both sides of a case, very active.
(III)	Has a stream of ideas, help from children, help from brothers, very careful conversationalist.
(IV)	Good education, happiness from children, good family life, pulls on successfully in his occupation.
(V)	Highly educated and intelligent, lucky children, gets unexpected chances in life for rise, influences through his talks.
(VI)	Troubled by enemies, broken education, has to spend on bad planning, much interested in sensual enjoyments.
(VII)	Good personality, hot temperament, happy married life, helpful children.
(VIII)	Loss of children possible, earns money in a very thoughtful manner.
(IX)	Good education, intelligent, diligent, good relations with brothers, has adjusting nature.
(X)	Good education, landed property, good businessman, domestic facilities, happy family.

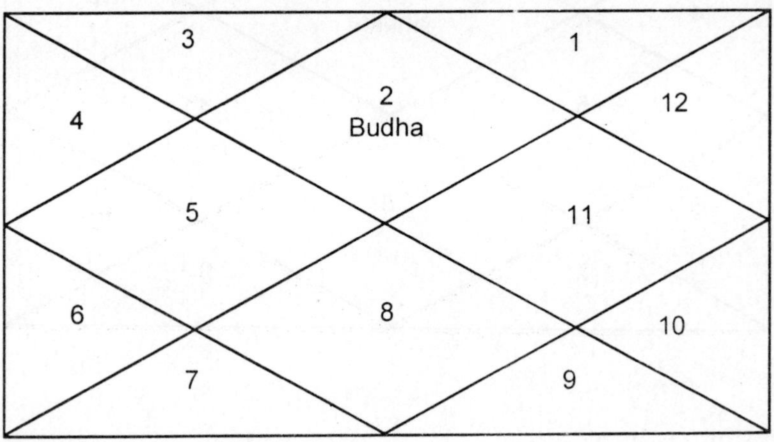

(XI) Earns through excessive labour, cannot earn to one's satisfaction, some problems from children, good earning after 32 years of life.

(XII) Heavy expenditure, problems from children some family problems.

Guru's Position in Vrishabha Lagna

House	Effects
(I)	Tendency of corporality, intelligence, religious minded wife, gains through legal means, creative thinking, smooth life.
(II)	Good accumulation of money, religious tendency.
(III)	Favoured by luck, steady income, good mannered wife.
(IV)	Some domestic problem, smooth working in the place of occupation, expenditure in suspicious work, devoted to God.
(V)	Easy success in efforts, steady income, healthy body and mind.
(VI)	Worries and obstacles, expenses more than income, spiritual progress, problems solved due to God's blessings.
(VII)	Good personality, easy and steady income, no windfall, good relations with brothers and sisters.
(VIII)	Longevity, philosophical tendency, fond of spending on religious works.
(IX)	Creative intelligence, helpful to others, good relations with brothers and sisters, success in efforts.
(X)	Very peaceful home environment, problems solved due to divine grace.
(XI)	Good income through lawful means, does not like to earn through immoral means.

(XII) Spiritual attitude, may try for liberation, saintly nature, good longevity.

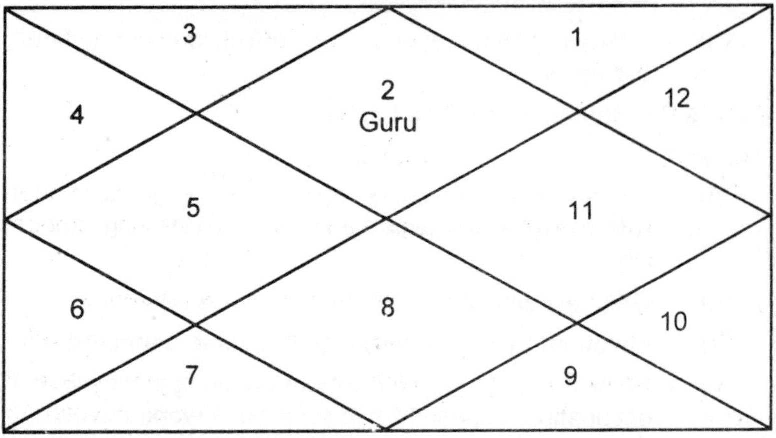

Shani's Position in Vrishabhȧ Lagna

House	Effects
(I)	Some bodily discomfort, colour black, laborious, some problems in the place of occupation, but gets popularity and success, some problem from wife, good relations with father.
(II)	Some dissatisfaction from home, wealth, through self-earning, may get father's favour, dissatisfaction from mother, some problems in property matters.
(III)	Very active and laborious, lucky and successful, some bodily problem possible, spends money carefully.
(IV)	Some problem of home and mother, non-smooth working in the place of occupation, difference of opinion from father, has to face difficulties in earning money.
(VI)	Differences with children, difficult earning, difference with wife, practical but harsh talk, accumulates money with difficulty.
(VII)	Differences with wife, unpeaceful home, bodily problem, obstacles in the rise of luck.
(VIII)	Longevity, good position in office, some problems from children.

(IX) Lucky, fortune favours after 36 years of age, lack of cordiality in relations with brother.

(X) Reaches high position in life, home front may not be very contented, differences with wife possible.

(XI) Huge earning, some problems of health, some differences with children.

(XII) Good earning and spending, obstacles in earning, overcomes enemies and obstacles.

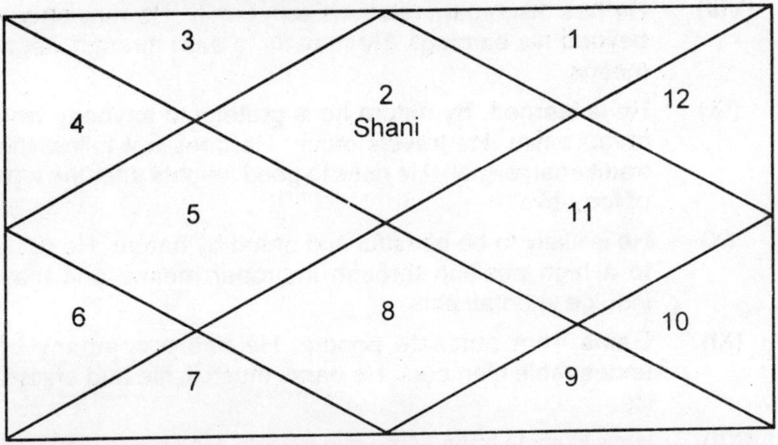

Rahu's Position in Vrishabha Lagna

House Effects

(I) A person having Rahu in the first house is likely to be cunning and works in crooked way. He is likely to be surrounded by women. He may excel in politics and subdues his enemies. He is likely to have a scar on his face.

(II) Talks in a harsh manner. Faces many obstacles in family life. He is likely to amass wealth through improper ways.

(III) He is quite active and successful. He entertains friendly feelings towards others. His enemies feel powerless before him.

(IV) He has a mother suffering from illnesses. His domestic life is not happy. He entertains many worries and evil plannings.

(V) He may get a son. He is likely to be timid. He has a sharp intellect, he has some differences of opinion with his progeny. One of the issues may abort.

(VI) He conquers his enemies. He is courageous and enjoys good health. He is not afraid of meeting any challenge from anybody.

(VII) His wife has imperfect health. Or she may be quarrelsome. He is likely to have dissatisfaction from his wife.

(VIII) He has discordant relations with family. He may spend beyond his earnings. He may try to earn through illegal means.

(IX) He is learned. By nature he is grateful to anybody who favours him. He travels much. He does not follow the traditional religion. He rises to good heights after the age of forty-two.

(X) He is likely to be boastful and proud by nature. He rises to a high position through improper means and may indulge in unfair acts.

(XI) Gains from outcaste people. He has a company of undesirable elements. He earns much in life and enjoys life.

(XII) He is likely to have some eye trouble. He scores victories over enemies. He spends on undesirable items.

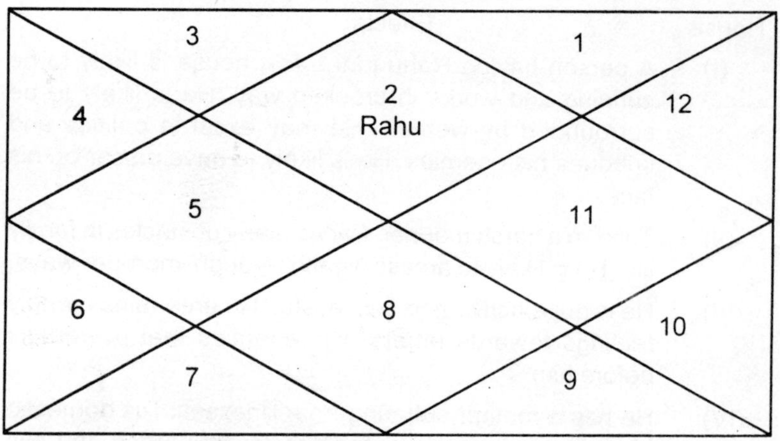

Ketu's Position in Vrishabha Lagna

House	Effects
(I)	The person shall be a lover of occult science. He gets general success and is amiable in nature.
(II)	His family life will be smooth and free from tensions.
(III)	Very active and successful. Makes progress through a thoughtful way.
(IV)	Family life may not be very peaceful. Does his work in a mysterious and silent manner.
(V)	He is diplomatic by nature and he has intriguing friends. Gets success through unusual manner and methodology.
(VI)	Vanquishes enemies and obstacles, through a planned thinking and manner.
(VII)	Wife a lover of mysterious cults. Obedient and mannerful wife.
(VIII)	Follower of mysterious cults. Is drawn towards the secret faiths.
(IX)	Makes rise through a constant struggle. Rises to a high position after the age of forty-six.
(X)	Gets success through a planned way. Can understand the plans of others and can safe-guard himself.
(XI)	The person has few friends. He gets help and gain from mysterious persons.
(XII)	Upsets the plans of enemies. Spends money on mysterious projects and faith.

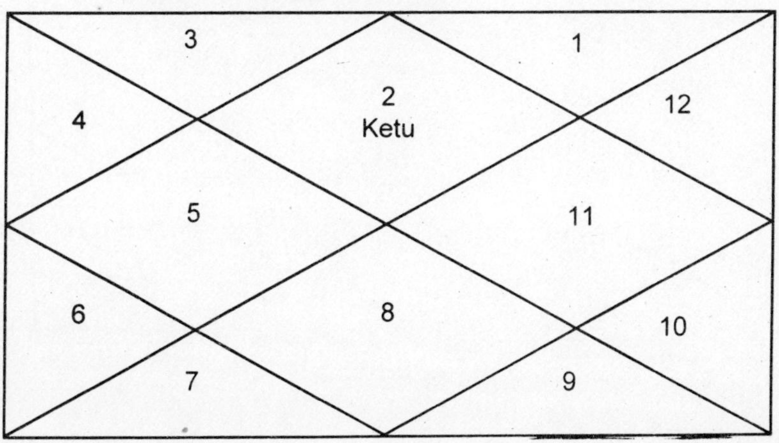

11

MITHUN LAGNA

Surya's Position in Mithuna Lagna

House	Effects
(I)	Love of travelling. There may be some problems concerning eyes. He is courageous and influential. He always gets prominent position wherever he works.
(II)	Fortunate. Spends money in good works. He may not have cordial relations with his relatives. He may be egoistic.
(III)	Very influential. Overcomes his enemies. Very forgiving by nature.
(IV)	Does not have a peaceful family. Heart is perturbed by the thoughts about enemies and their actions.
(V)	Gets disappointment from his eldest son. He has sharp political wisdom and intellect.
(VI)	He is a terror to his enemies. Over spends his earnings.
(VII)	One is unhappy due to the temperament of ones wife. Does not have sweet relations with her.
(VIII)	He is likely to be deceitful. He has beautiful body. He is cheated by women. He can be a seeker of metaphysical wisdom.
(IX)	He is fortunate, influential and dashing. He may get very big positions due to his courageous works.
(X)	The person gets high position in the place he works. He has good relations with superior authorities. He gets the blessings of his father.

(XI) Gets ample riches. He may not get sufficient satisfaction from his progeny. He has very influential and powerful friends who are always ready to help him.

(XII) He may have some eye trouble. He always wins over his enemies. He does not follow traditional religion.

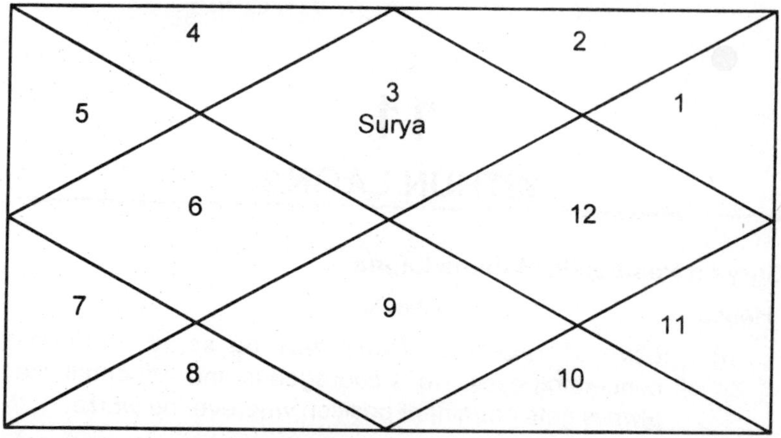

Chandra's Position in Mithuna Lagna

House	Effects
(I)	Strong, happy and has a long life. Wife is likely to be beautiful and obedient.
(II)	Prosperous, has a big family, intelligent, having good reputation.
(III)	Very popular with ladies, fond of light literature, poetry, wealth.
(IV)	Gets the pleasure of conveyance, popular with the ruling persons, has the advantage of good residential houses.
(V)	Good intelligence, popularity, has many progenies, has a loving wife.
(VI)	Overcomes his enemies, has a number of enemies, has to make a lot of efforts for the rise of fortune.
(VII)	Easily attracted towards opposite sex, kind-hearted, beautiful personality, lovable by nature, enjoys the pleasure of living in palatial houses.

(VIII) Full of worries, is not happy from his family, can get everything through religious practice.

(IX) Very fortunate. People are full of praise for him, has religious bent of mind and is fortunate.

(X) Religious temperament, respected by the person with whom he works, is able to achieve his life's ambitions.

(XI) Enjoys excellent reputation, gets prestige, money and love of people, never has any shortage of money, surrounded by girl friends.

(XII) Spends money on religious ceremonies, is terrorized by enemies, has few friends.

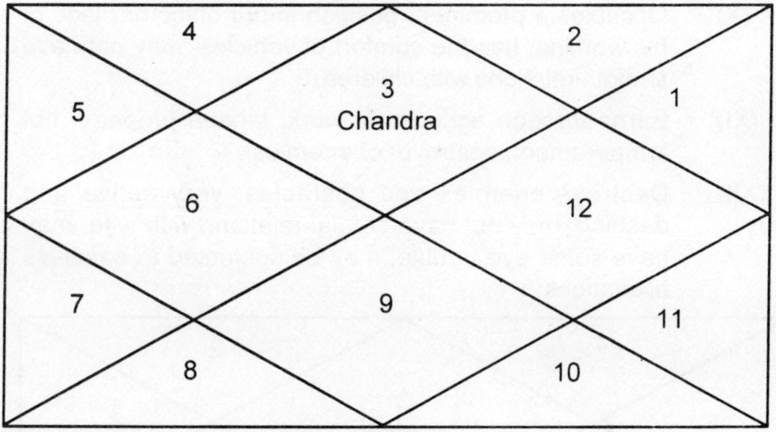

Mangal's Position in Mithuna Lagna

House Effects

(I) May have headache, cruel, brave, may have medical operation, disharmony in relations with wife.

(II) Shall amass wealth through improper ways, may not have very cordial relations with the members of his family, may lose one of the progenies through abortion. Hot tempered.

(III) Very active and victorious, dashing, earns through fearless manner, makes rise after the age of 28 years of age.

(IV) Does not have domestic felicity, may profit by landed property, may have a quarrelsome wife, may earn through inflammable items like petrol, gas, etc.

(V) May have an aborted child, may not have smooth relations with children, may have a very practical attitude of life.

(VI) Destroyer of enemies, may have some surgical problem, spends on landed property.

(VII) May not get happiness from wife, some problems in marriage, not good for health.

(VIII) May have problems from relatives, family life full of strife, very active.

(IX) Earns money through self-effort, rises after the age of 28, worshipper of a deity of power like Hanuman or Kali.

(X) Occupies a prominent position in the office or place of his working, has the comfort of vehicles, may not have smooth relations with children.

(XI) Earns through agricultural work, landed property, hot temperament, destroyer of enemies.

(XII) Destroys enemies and obstacles, very active and dashing, may not have cordial-relations with wife, may have some eye trouble, may be subjected to baseless allegations.

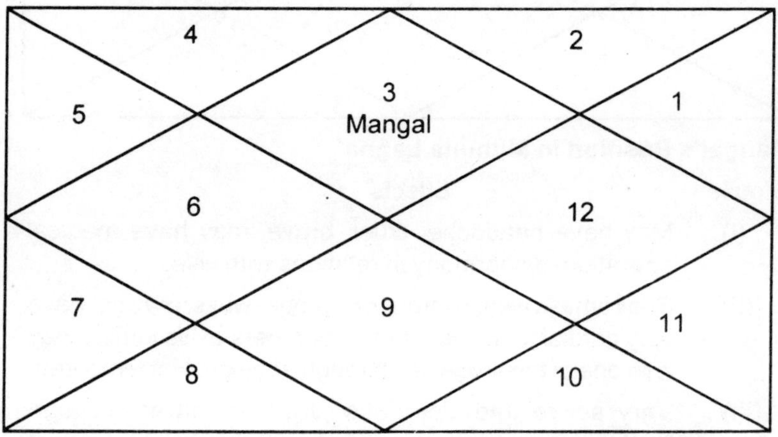

Position of Shukra in Mithuna Lagna

House	Effects
(I)	Very charming personality. Practical outlook. Wife beautiful. Loves luxuries of life. Spends heavily on luxuries.
(II)	Beautiful face. Happy family. Savings become possible only if luxuries are curtailed. Good education. Liked by people.
(III)	Good relation with brothers especially with sisters. Progeny brings money. Unexpected chances of betterment in life.
(IV)	Dissatisfaction from children. Otherwise generally speaking good conditions at home.
(V)	Progeny extremely helpful and the births of children likely to bring good luck. Very polite speech. Diplomatic nature.
(VI)	Troubled by enemies, but comes out successful from conflicts, victorious due to diplomatic mind.
(VII)	Charming personality. Smooth relations with wife. Wife more interested in materialistic life than in spiritual matters.
(VIII)	Materialistic attitude. Happy married life. Good relations with the members of family.
(IX)	Gets some unexpected opportunity for betterment. Children bring luck. Good rise in life, especially after the age of thirty-six.
(X)	Very good position in the field of activity. Very happy home. All facilities of good residence and vehicles. Popular and successful in life.
(XI)	Good relations with children. Children helpful even from the stand-point of economic life. Some member of fair sex proves very helpful.

(XIII) Successful material life. Enjoys life on a grand scale. Purely materialistic life.

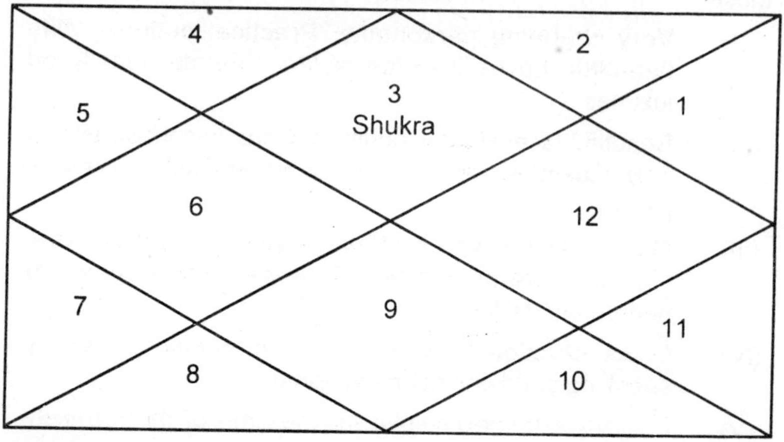

Budha in Mithuna Lagna

House	Effects
(I)	Beautiful bodily build, clever and wise, practical, fond of learning, lover of literature, soft speech, learned.
(II)	Intelligent and wealthy, happy family, art of speech making, earns respect from one and all.
(III)	Having friendship with the people connected with business world, loved by brothers, good journalist, gets his work done in an amicable way.
(IV)	Has a peaceful and prosperous family, enjoys good influence in the ruling class, has a number of vehicles and houses, has a contented life.
(V)	Has some girl issues, possesses practical intelligence, earns money through intelligent planning.
(VI)	Overcomes his enemies, has a tendency of renunciation, is good in the art of arguing, learned and opposes the ruling party.
(VII)	Has a very beautiful wife, has many sons, very practical in approach, very tactful, and has a good personality.

(VIII) Has a long life, may get an international recognition, may become a judicial officer, follows religion in a practical way.

(IX) Learned, writer of books, helpful to the needy, increases the reputation of his family.

(X) Has ancestral wealth, gets political power, speaks only when necessary, earns good amount of money and has a smooth career.

(XI) Earns ample amount of wealth, makes a large number of friends through his sweet temperament, leads a luxurious life, can become a good political leader through his oratorial power.

(XII) Spends money on good projects, helpful to the needy, has a fickle mind, love of learning.

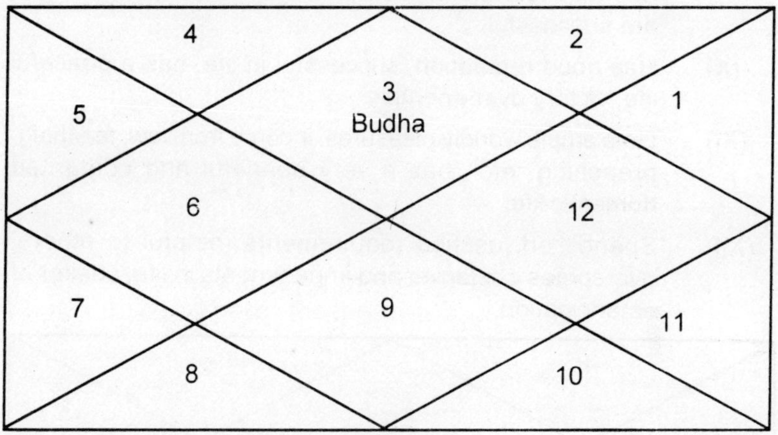

Guru's Position in Mithuna Lagna

House Effects

(I) Good bodily build, healthy, lover of knowledge, has a very lucky wife, has good progenies, fortunate, religious minded.

(II) Very satisfied family life, may occupy a post of power, speaks softly, avoids conflicts, beautiful and obedient wife, may become an efficient teacher, preacher, judge, etc., is likely to enjoy reputation.

(III) Has a steady means of income, fortunate, has happiness from wife and her relatives.

(IV) Has some domestic problem, successful in profession, religious minded, spends on piety, charity, etc.

(V) Very fortunate, no problems in money earning, sincere and Satvik in thinking.

(VI) Tendency of renunciation, destroyer of enemies, ill health, fond of making pilgrimages.

(VII) Earning from good sources, enjoys state honour, has a number of helpful friends.

(VIII) Long life, philosophic tendency, fond of religious discussion, lover of liberation, leads a Satvik life.

(IX) Has number of sons, gets reputation, has Satvik thinking, has good relations with brothers, efforts to improve fortune are successful.

(X) Has good reputation, successful in life, has a peaceful life, victory over enemies.

(XI) Gets ample worldly pleasures, income from law, teaching, preaching, etc., has a very peaceful and contented domestic life.

(XII) Spends on justified requirements, helpful to others, overcomes obstacles and impediments in life, seeker of emancipation.

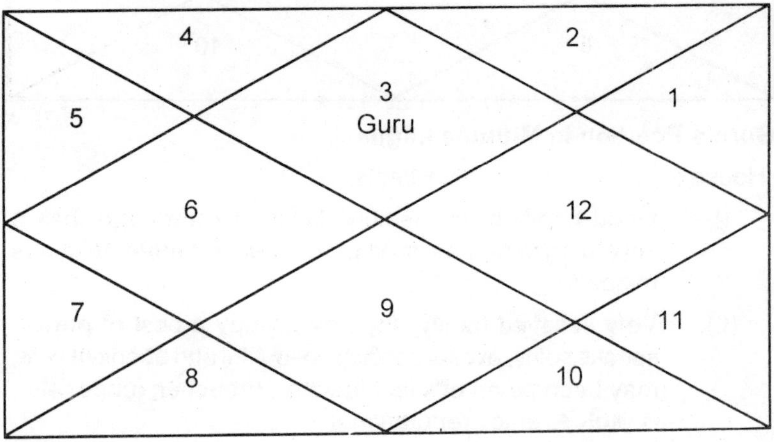

Shani's Position in the Mithuna Lagna

House	Effects
(I)	Destroyer of enemies and obstacles, some problems from wife, some obstacles in working. Rises after the age of 36. Popular amongst the common men.
(II)	May go away from home for earning money. Hard speech, wealthy, disharmonious relations with the relatives.
(III)	Very active, self-made personality, hard working, liberal, intelligent. Gets fame.
(IV)	May not get mother's happiness. May have unsatisfactory domestic life. Overcomes enemies. Problems in the place of working.
(V)	May not have helpful friends. Obstacles in education. May not get satisfaction from his progeny. May not do well with wife.
(VI)	Puts down enemies and obstacles. Fearless. Gets recognition and help from government.
(VII)	Dissatisfaction from family. Problems from wife, struggles for earning livelihood.
(VIII)	Longevity. Ascetic tendency. Can make progress in spiritual direction.
(IX)	Very fortunate. Good fortune after a struggle. Good rise after the age of 36 years. May have a tendency of renunciation.
(X)	Gets honour from people. Gets recognition from the government. Miserly habits. Unhappy family life. Disagreement with wife on many issues.
(XI)	Earning from oil or iron. May not have many friends. But they are reliable. Thoughtful. Some problems from progeny. Generally speaking, wealthy and successful in the later age of life.

(XII) Never surrenders to the enemies. Overcomes them. Leader of people. May spend on undesirable items. Follows thoughtful religion instead of following traditional path.

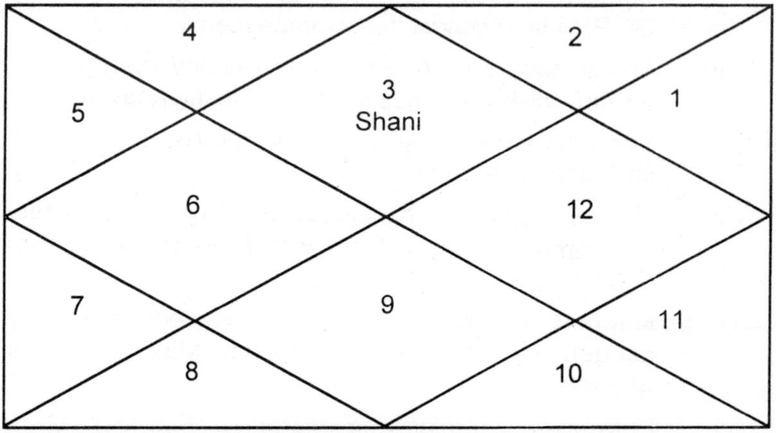

Rahu's Position in Mithuna Lagna

House	Effects
(I)	Subduer of enemies. Practical. Achieves his objective through fair or foul means. On the whole, he is truthful and does not go against his words.
(II)	Possibility of false behaviour, Boastful. Domestic life full of dissension.
(III)	Very powerful. Has good feelings towards all. Gains victory over obstacles and enemies. Courageous, successful. May prosper in a foreign land.
(IV)	Diseased mother. Lacks peaceful domestic life. Possibility of some problems in family.
(V)	Gets son. Surrounded by worries. Sharp intelligence. Lacks sweet speech.
(VI)	Overcomes enemies and obstacles. Has a lot of patience. Defeats intrigues of others.
(VII)	May have an ill wife. Wife quarrelsome. May indulge in sinful acts.

(VIII) Very laborious. Useless travelling. Distressful family life. Follows irrational religion.

(IX) Learned. Respected by people. May have relations with an inferior lady. Capable of attaining his objective through any means. May follow Tamasik religion.

(X) Egoistic temperament. Is not afraid of opposing anybody on a rational ground. Family life unhappy. May attain political heights.

(XI) Gains money from persons belonging to non-Hindu communities. Earns much wealth by following non-fair means too. Rise after the age of forty-two.

(XII) May have some eye problem. May spend money on unfair items. May not follow traditional religion. May settle in some foreign land.

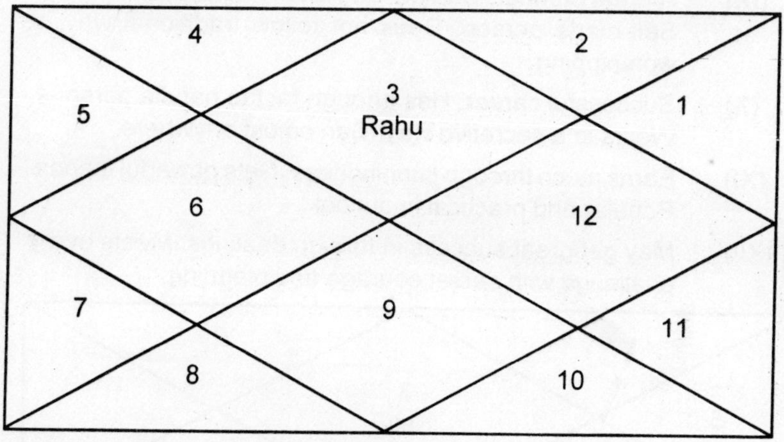

Ketu's Position in Mithuna Lagna

House	Effects
(I)	A lover of mystic science. Good health. Tactful. Has a good and cooperative wife. Rise after the age of 46 years of life.
(II)	Mental restlessness. Some problems of family. Love for untraditional religion. Frank and outspoken. There may be some eye trouble.
(III)	Very active and energetic. Makes rise through one's own secret planning. Gets popularity. General success.

(IV) Some domestic upheaval. Unhelpful family. Tactful handling of matter.

(V) Loves mystic lore. Soft-speaking. Intelligent. Does not reveal his mind. There may be some problems concerning progeny.

(VI) Conquers enemies through tact. Not afraid of obstacles. Is not boastful. Believes in doing work without any publicity.

(VII) Intelligent wife. Wife may be quarrelsome to some extent. But she is helpful in the material progress.

(VIII) A love for esotoric science. Does not get any inheritance. Members of the family may not be very helpful in life.

(IX) A great planner. Can get success in diplomatic service. Self-made person. Does not follow traditional way of worshipping.

(X) Successful career. Has enough tact to handle persons. Works in a secretive way. Can adjust anywhere.

(XI) Earns much through cunningness. Gets powerful friends. Popular and practical in outlook.

(XII) May get great success in foreign dealings. Meets every challenge with secret courage and planning.

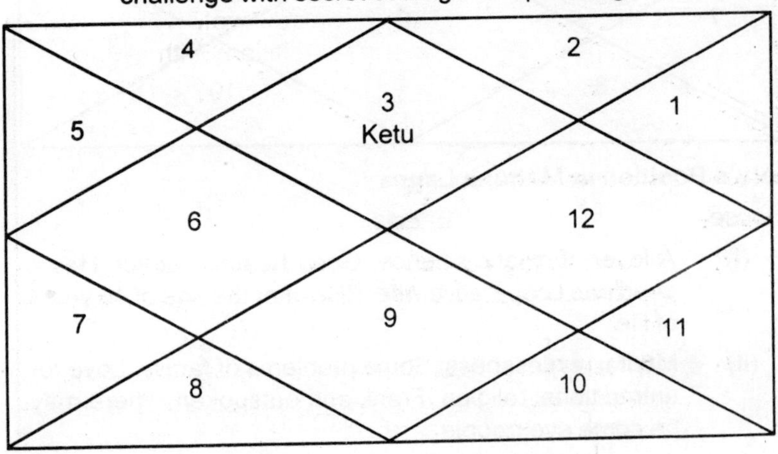

12

KARKA LAGNA

Positions of Surya in Karka Lagna

House	Effects
(I)	Fluctuating fortune. Some problems in marriage. Believes in returning the behaviour meted out to him in the same coin. Hot temperament.
(II)	Accumulates ample riches. Influential family. Gets much name and fame.
(III)	Very practical and active. Defeats his enemies. Has an access in the government. Can gain from political life.
(IV)	Domestic problems. Cannot pull well with higher authorities. May not have good relations with members of family. Gets importance where he works.
(V)	Cold speech. Abortive tendency of wife. Gets unexpected rise in life. Critical faculty developed.
(VI)	Puts down his enemies. Succeeds despite all odds. Dashing and fearless. Can prove to be a good leader.
(VII)	Some problems from wife. Hot temperament. Subdues opposition. May lose in business partnership.
(VIII)	Accumulates huge amount of money. Impresses through conversation. Boastful. Favoured by father.
(IX)	Very prosperous. Lucky. Courageous. Influential. Powerful. An outstanding person in his personal family.
(X)	Very influential. Occupies some prominent position in the field of his activity.

(XI) Earns from government and through association with high personalities. Very wealthy and lives a pompus life.

(XII) Spends excessively, quells opposition. Proves a good administrative head.

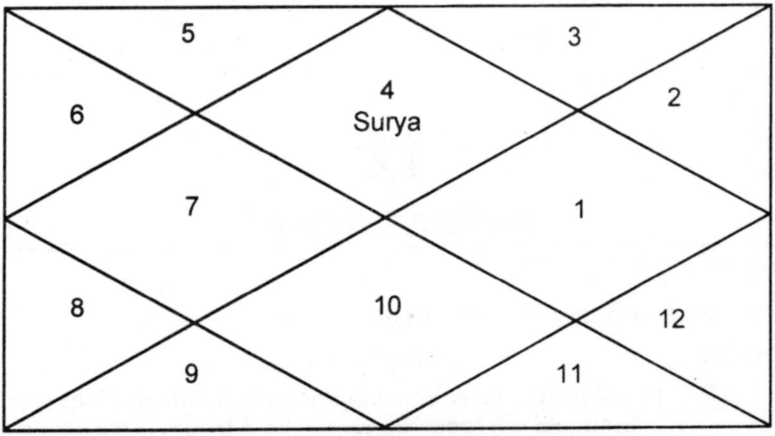

Chandrama's Positions in Karka Lagna

House	Effects
(I)	Handsome personality. Delicate. Soft-speaking. White complexion. Changing moods. Magnanimous heart.
(II)	Happy family. Congenial atmosphere in family. Amiable temperament.
(III)	Practical outlook. Diplomatic. Good relations with brothers and sisters. Many plans in mind. Active and agile.
(IV)	Balanced view of life. Very happy domestic life. Loving mother. Happiness of conveyances.
(V)	Sickly constitution. Sweet tongued. Unexpected gains in life. Intelligent. Highly excitable.
(VI)	Sickly constitution. Has to be careful about his health throughout life. Lives in a danger of enemies. Overcomes obstacles through faith in God.
(VII)	Beautiful personality. Beautiful wife. Sentimental nature. Religious minded.
(VIII)	Happy family life. Never feels insulted from family. Wife brings money, i.e., rise after marriage.

(IX) Very fortunate. Very religious minded. Very lucky. Very popular. Very sweet-tongued person.

(X) Boastful but successful. Gets excited at a slight provocation. Good at heart. Liked by the friends and the persons where he works.

(XI) Excellent health. Joyous temperament. Gets benefit from the opposite sex. May be expert in music or a great lover of music. Liked by the opposite sex.

(XII) Weak constitution. Practical thinking. Over spends money. May like to go to some foreign land.

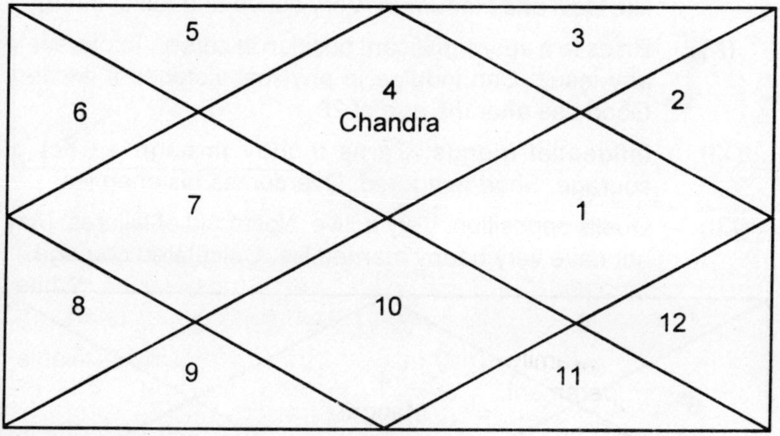

Mangal's Positions in Karka Lagna

House	Effects
(I)	Hot temperament. Some problems from wife. Some problem from the progeny. May get advantages of property and conveyances. Rise in life with self-help.
(II)	Earns much through painstaking effort. Influential family. Gets sudden and unexpected chances for the betterment of fortune. Abortion of a child possible.
(III)	Very active and influential. Dashing. Successful career. Rises to top position in the hierarchy of officers.
(IV)	Some domestic trouble indicated. Absence of harmony between wife and husband. Good rise in career. Earns through property business.

(V) Male children. One abortion possible. Courageous. Intelligent. Makes way through opposition and struggle.

(VI) Suppresses every opposition. Some surgical problem in body. Fearless attitude. Worship of deities like Devi or Hanuman.

(VII) Rises to the top position in career. Hot temperament. Very courageous and powerful. Can prove to be a first class administrator.

(VIII) Married life may not be happy. Earns through good chances in life. Influential friends.

(IX) Very courageous. Faith in the worship of gods of strength like Devi and Hanuman. Very active and full of energy.

(X) Rises to a very significant position in career. Intolerent to any insult. Can indulge in physical violence if excited. Good rise after the age of 28.

(XI) Influential friends. Earns money through an act of courage. Short tempered. Overcomes his enemies.

(XII) Quells opposition. Very active. Not afraid of failures. May not have very happy married life. Calculated courage.

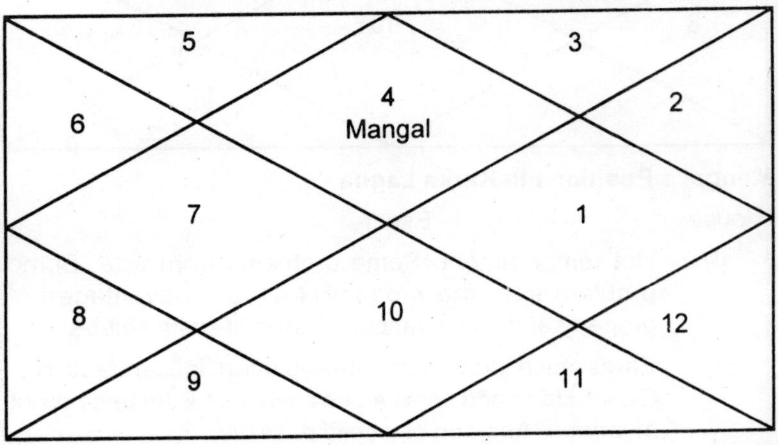

Shukra's Positions in Karka Lagna

House	Effects
(I)	Handsome personality. Beautiful wife. Good source of income. Happy domestic life. Popular amongst the opposite sex. Aesthetic sense developed. Lover of music or art.
(II)	Amasses good amount of wealth. Happy family life. Helpful family. May get good legacy.
(III)	Active. But efforts take long time to fructify. Good fortune through a member of opposite sex. Earns through self-effort.
(IV)	Enjoyment of fine house and conveyance facilities. Very cordial atmosphere in the family. Graceful in behaviour. May lead a very comfortable life.
(V)	Quarrelsome friends. Some hindrances in income. Number of girl progenies more than the male progeny. Tactful. Windsome speech. Some problems of family.
(VI)	A life of struggle. Many handicaps. Spends much on luxuries. Tactful handling of enemies. Graceful behaviour even with enemies.
(VII)	Handsome personality. Beautiful wife. Cooperative members in family. Domestic comforts. Rise after marriage likely.
(VIII)	Illness due to excessive indulgence in sensual pleasures. Happy family life. No dearth of money.
(IX)	Very lucky. Gets easy success in efforts. A member of opposite sex may be very helpful in the rise of fortune. Remarkable income.
(X)	Tactful. Popular. Easy going in profession. Happy domestic life. Enjoyment of conveyances and residence.
(XI)	Very good income. Help from a member of opposite sex. Very comfortable family life. Facilities of good residential house and conveyances.

(XII) Overspends on luxuries. Faces enemies tactfully. May be in trouble because of a member of opposite sex. Some problems of family.

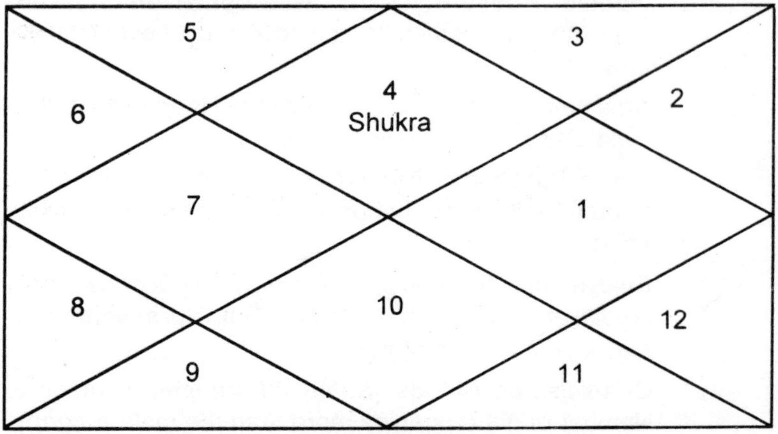

Budha's Positions in Karka Lagna

House	Effects
(I)	Spendthrift. Practical. Has many plannings. Always thinks about improving his position in career-making.
(II)	Difficulty in amassing wealth. Capable of taking risk in business. Harmonious family life.
(III)	Very practical. Gets success through very practical planning. Commercial intelligence sharp.
(IV)	Happy family life. Takes due care about the welfare of every member of the family. May be worried about expenses beyond expectation.
(V)	Very intelligent. Tries to cash every opportunity that comes in his life. The number of daughters likely to be more than male issues.
(VI)	Worried by the failures. May be worried because of enemies. But solves his problems through practical attitude.
(VII)	Beautiful and practical wife or husband. Good personality. Leaning towards doing business.
(VIII)	Peaceful family. Sweet talking. Not much interested in religion.

(IX) Makes progress through constant effort and foresight. Gets easy success.

(X) Very practical and adjusting in nature. Can prove very popular with his co-workers. Peaceful domestic life.

(XI) Makes fortune through practical planning. Many friends who help. Help from brothers too. Liked by his associates due to fine nature.

(XII) Spends money cautiously. Deals with opposition without any worry. Has a good way of handling an obstacle or opposition.

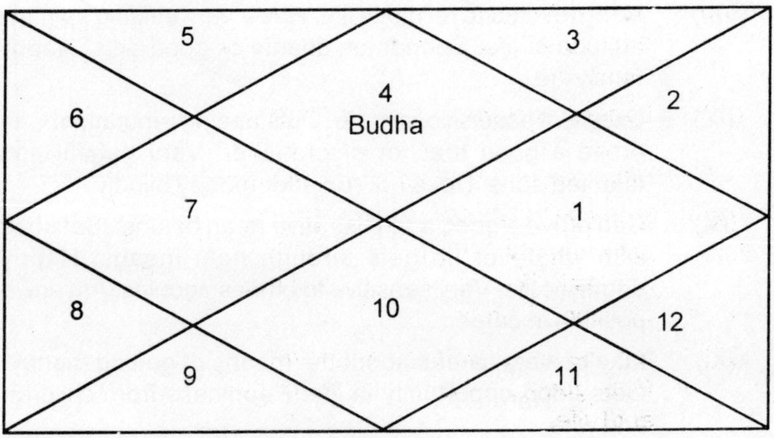

Guru's Positions in Karka Lagna

House Effects

(I) Charming personality. Remarkable religious taste. Cheerful. Obedient and cooperative wife. Gets easy success in life. Makes a slow but very steady progress in life.

(II) Happy family life. Religious atmosphere in family. Extraordinary faith in religious life. Spiritual attitude dominates. Helpful atmosphere in the field of career.

(III) Very active, but a man of principles. Good rise from the age of 16. Unselfish. Helpful to others. Good reputation.

(IV) Some domestic problem. Religious attitude of life. Spends on good items and religious performances. May visit many religious places.

(V) Gets an excellent chance in life. Sons dutiful and helpful. One of the sons may bring outstanding reputation. Never forsakes one's religious principles for the sake of money.

(VI) Few enemies. Enjoys reputation even in the field of enemies. Spends on charity and religious performances. Good family atmosphere. Earns money through virtuous acts.

(VII) Lacks religious zeal. Very thoughtful and logical in pursuing religious faith. May be harassed by enemies sometime in life. Follows no principles in earning money. Good personality.

(VIII) Very devoted to religious life. Has a very abiding spiritual attitude in life. Spends on charity or good acts. Happy family life.

(IX) Excellent acquisitions in life. Outstanding reputation. Can prove a good teacher or preacher. Very helpful and talented sons. Does not run after money blindly.

(X) Can prove a good administrative head or jurist. Satisfied with whatever he gets through right means. Happy domestic life. Very sensitive to other's agonies. Assertive position in career.

(XI) May be very careful about the means of getting money. Gets good opportunity in life. Happiness from children and wife.

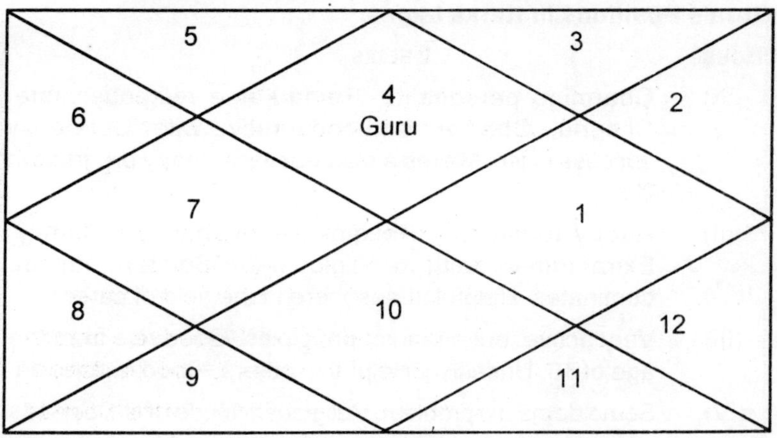

(XII) Has a desire for religious attainments. Aims at getting emancipation. Free from enemies and oppositions.

Shani's Position in Karka Lagna

House	Effects
(I)	Problems of health. Problems from wife. Thoughtful. A tendency of renunciation. Philosophical attitude towards life.
(II)	Family life disturbed. Lack of harmony in the members of family. Difference of opinion between son and father. Comfort of conveyances. Earns through struggle and competition.
(III)	Very active. Popular. Rise after initial struggles. Philosophical temperament. Spends money after due consideration.
(IV)	Life partner comes from a higher circle of society. Rise in life after marriage. Longevity.
(V)	Problems from children. At least one child is lost through abortion. Harsh tone of speech. Some differences with wife. No harmony in family life.
(VI)	Conquers enemies. Not afraid of calamities and opposition. Not swayed by the fear of enemies. Some problems possible in service.
(VII)	Very fortunate life-partner. Some problems of health possible. Has to pass through struggles for betterment. Rise after the age of 36 possible.
(VIII)	Good longevity of life. Philosophical temperament. No peace in the place of working. Differences with children or problems concerning them.
(IX)	Very active. Popular. Follows a religion based on rational insight. Earns money after 36. Life partner helpful directly or indirectly.
(X)	Problems of family. Married life not very happy. Builds houses and land property through constant effort and labour. Problems in the field of career.
(XI)	Good income after marriage. Helpful partner. Some problems concerning health. Children not obedient.

(XII) Struggles but wins ultimately. A man of careful thought. Very rational view of religion. Not afraid of hardships. No happy relation with parents and family.

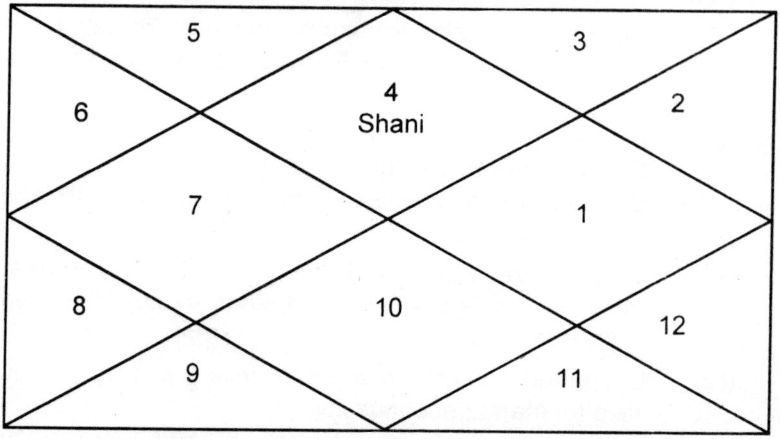

Rahu's Positions in Karka Lagna

House	Effects
(I)	Mind is attacked by destructive thoughts. Tendency to turn in improper directions. Some scar on face. Somewhat disturbed relations with wife. Masters opposition and intrigues.
(II)	Uneasy family ties. Destructive use of power. Non-congenial relations with father. Gets success in political field. Has good influence in official circle.
(III)	Very active and successful. Very practical. Gets success through careful panning. Has to struggle for reaching higher positions.
(IV)	Some problems in family. Gets conveyance and property through diplomatic tactics.
(V)	One of the children is lost through abortion. Destructive and quarrelsome tendency. Gets opportunities for rising to unexpected heights.
(VI)	Subdues enemies and opposition. Rise through struggles. Expenditure on destructive habits.

(VII) Helpful wife. Some possibility of ill health and accident through conveyance. Popularity in foreign land possible if an attempt is made.

(VIII) Faith in Tamasik religious faiths. Difference with father and family. Should be careful while driving any vehicle.

(IX) Does not follow Satvik religion. May be interested in Tantras and Mantras. Makes rise through fair or foul means.

(X) Some problems in the field of working. Possibilities of oppositions and intrigues. Boldness of handling every situation. Rise through struggles and competitions.

(XI) Unusually high income. Friendship with undesirable elements. Possibility of foreign friends.

(XII) Spendthrift. May visit foreign land. Scores victories over enemies of all sorts.

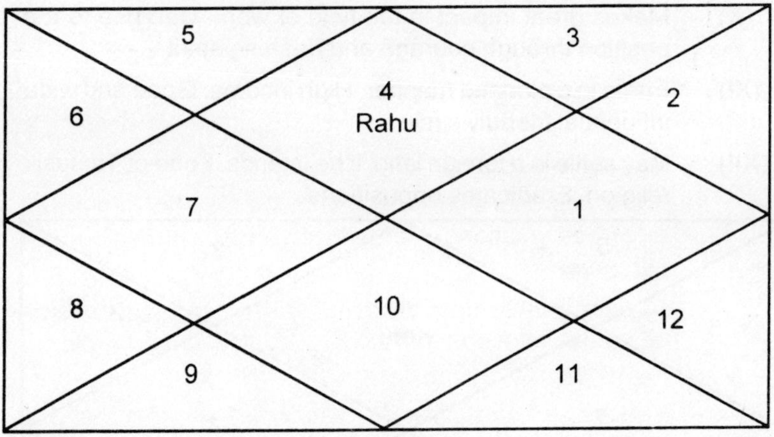

Positions of Ketu in Karka Lagna

House Effects

(I) A good planning ability. Practical in outlook. Mentally alert. Cunningness.

(II) Brings glory to family. But relations with the members of family may not be smooth. A great diplomatic capacity.

(III) Very active. Practical. Relations with brothers may not be very harmonious. Rises in life through skilful planning.

(IV) Gets luxuries of landed property and conveyances. But there may be some problems in family life.

(V) Boldness in approach. Not afraid of any opposition. Some problems concerning children. Exploits every opportunity of making worldly progress.

(VI) Suppresses opposition in a diplomatic manner. Makes a practical plan for humbling enemies.

(VII) Very helpful wife. Relations with wife may not be very harmonious. Some problems of health possible.

(VIII) Interest in black religion. Mysterious religions attract the person. Family life may not be up to the mark.

(IX) Makes great strides in life through careful planning. Is not particular in choosing the right means. Motto is "Nothing succeeds like success".

(X) Makes great impact in the field of work. Can rise to top position through courage and dashing spirit.

(XI) Earns in a planned manner. High income. Good and wide influential friendly circle.

(XII) May settle in a foreign land, if he intends. Fond of Tamasik religion. Eradicates oppositions.

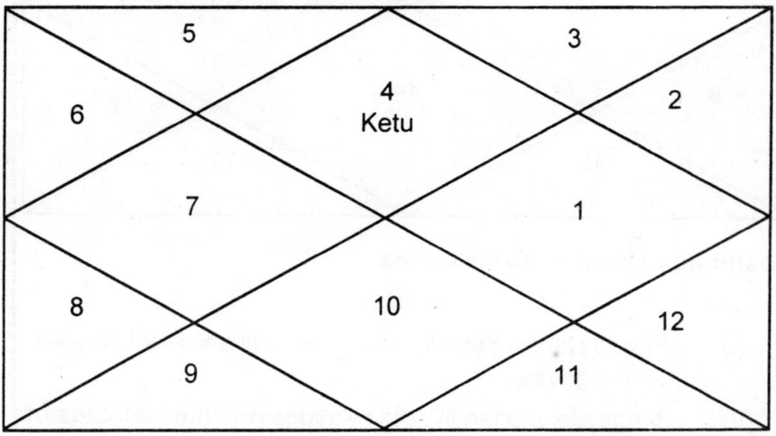

13

SIMHA LAGNA

Surya's Positions in Simha Lagna

House	Effects
(I)	Impressive personality. Egoistic. Man of principles. Courageous. Cannot adjust with everybody. Some problems in marriage.
(II)	Practical. No coordination in family. Hard speech. Wealthy. Religious minded.
(III)	Very laborious. Successful. Rise in life due to the influence or help of any influential person or relative.
(IV)	Suffers from some family problem. Has ample residential facilities and conveyances. Occupies an important position in the domain of his field of activity.
(V)	Very fortunate. Gets unexpected chances in life. Has sons who occupy important positions in life. Differences with progeny. Very intelligent.
(VI)	Subdues enemies and oppositions. Very helpful to friends. There may be some health problems. Attains good reputation in life.
(VII)	May have some ailing tendency. But on the whole has strong health. Temperament is hot. May not have very cordial relations with life-partner.
(VIII)	May not have very happy family life. Has interest in spiritual matters. Learned. May have weak health.
(IX)	Very fortunate. Earns prestige and position through self-effort. Interested in spiritual religion as against traditional religion.

(X) Gets very high position in the domain of his field of activity. Can shine even in the domain of politics, if interested. Has pleasures of good residential houses and conveyances. May not have happy family life.

(XI) Earns money in extraordinary quantity. Has helpful friends. Occupies influential position in ruling elite. May not have very cordial relations with progeny.

(XII) May have some eye trouble. Conquers enemies. Follows a religion of his own rational thinking. Vanquishes enemies. May become a spend-thrift. Some health problems too are possible.

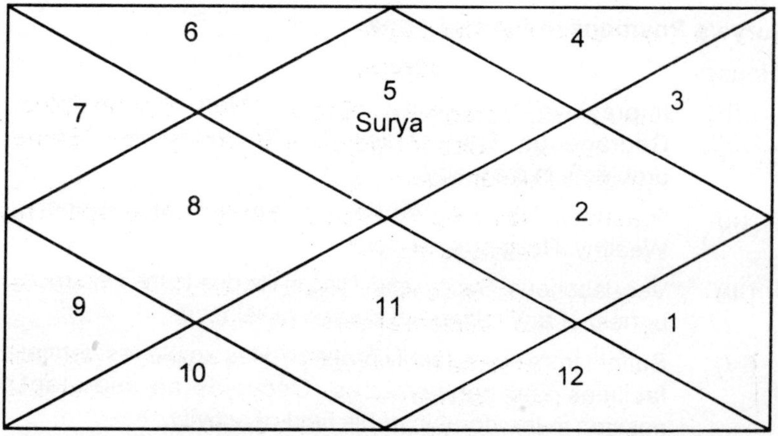

Chandrama's Positions in Simha Lagna

House Effects

(I) Good personality. Courageous. Man of determination. Expensive habits. Beautiful and devoted wife.

(II) Practical attitude. Good personality. Happy family life. Soft spoken. Expenses more than the income.

(III) Artistic temperament. Balanced outlook and behaviour. Good relations with brothers and sisters. Easy success in life.

(IV) Some domestic problems. Pessimistic outlook. Problems regarding mother.

(V) Very religious minded. Good intelligence. Obedient children. May get one unexpected chance of betterment in life.

(VI) Persecuted by enemies and expenses. But a person of fortitude and patience.

(VII) Beautiful wife. Beautiful personality. Lovable in nature. Keeps secrets his inner thoughts.

(VIII) Religious in nature. Happy family. Long life. Pleasing speech. Cannot save much money in life.

(IX) Courageous. Frank in speech. Full of enthusiasm. Make rise with the cooperation of others. Enjoys popularity.

(X) Very happy and prosperous family life. Enjoys advantages of good residences and conveyances. Popularity. Smooth working in the field of activity.

(XI) Expenditure more than income. Worried about extra means of earning money. Very big sphere of friendship. Popular amongst the opposite sex.

(XII) Faith in religious pursuits. Undertakes a number of travellings. Chances of going away from home and settling there. Cares much for mother and gets her blessings.

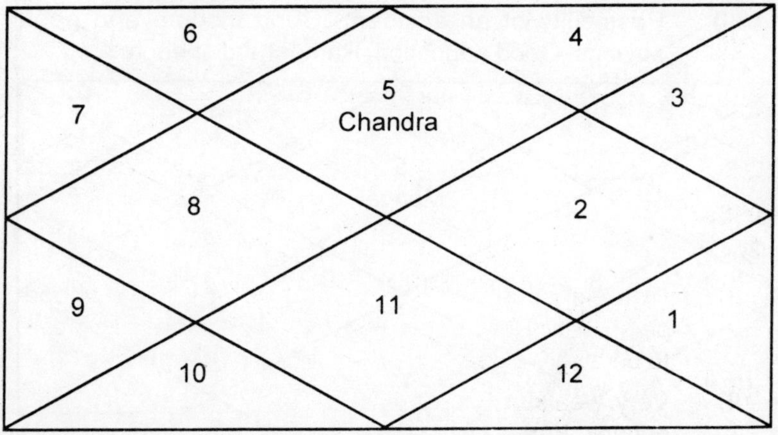

Mangala's Positions in Simha Lagna

House Effects

(I) Very fortunate. A deep sense of ego. Very courageous. Self-confident. Makes very good rise in life after the age of twenty-eight.

(II) Moderate courage. Some problems of family. Good savings. Fortunate. Can reach one's destination of success despite odds.

(III) Non-smooth relations with brothers. Generally unprovoked, but if provoked, one shall not mind going to the extreme.

(IV) Home full of facilities. Enough landed property. But still there may be discontent.

(V) Very fortunate progeny. Danger of abortion. Helpful friends. Courageous. Dogmatic attitude of religion.

(VI) Overcomes one's enemies and impediments. Marches to success through struggles. Life rises in a higher ladder of success after the age of twenty-eight.

(VII) Delay in marriage. Adjustment with wife becomes rather difficult. Prominent position in the field of working. Hot tempered.

(VIII) Possibility of an accident. Good income and good savings. Good education. Rather hard speech.

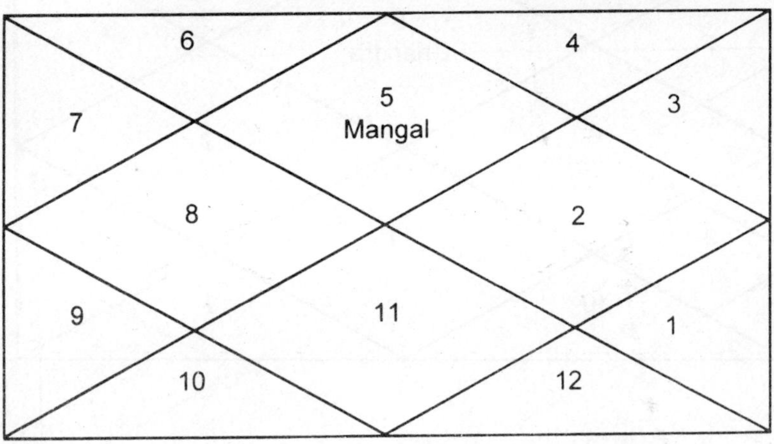

(IX) Very fortunate. A higher turn of success after twenty-eight years of age.

(X) Prominent position in the field of working. Danger of abortion. Hot tempered.

(XI) Very good income. Commands a good circle of friends. Good savings. Helpful friends and children.

(XII) Fond of travelling. Travelling brings good fortune. May settle in some foreign land.

Positions of Shukra in Simha Lagan

House	Effects
(I)	Handsome personality. Beautiful wife. Influential position in the field of work. Energetic and active.
(II)	Good family atmosphere. One tries to be very active. But efforts are not always successful. Weak position in the field of work.
(III)	Very active and successful. Progressive positions in the field of work. Rises by dint of self-effort in life.
(IV)	Happy domestic life. Important position in the field of career. Comforts of good residential houses and conveyances.
(V)	Helped by friends belonging to the opposite sex. First issue may be a girl. Popularity in the opposite sex circle.

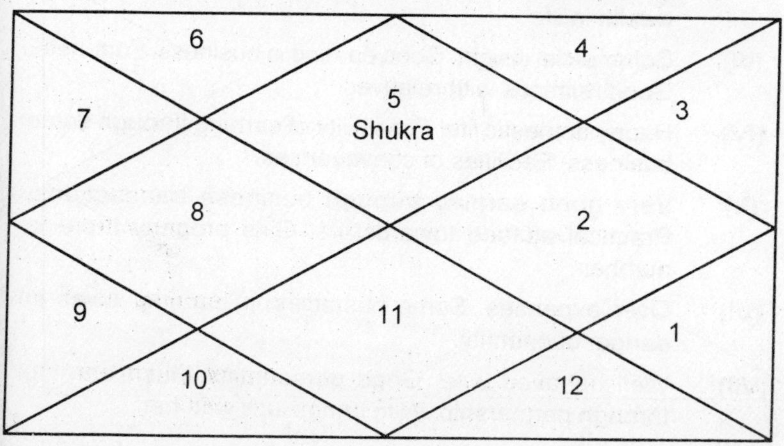

(VI) Heavy expenses on luxuries. Difficulties in the place of working. Tactful handling of enemies and difficulties.

(VII) Beautiful personality. Beautiful life partner. Helped by the luck of the life-partner.

(VIII) Happy and cooperative family. Materialistic attitude. Rises to higher positions in life through one's own efforts.

(IX) Very active and zestful. Efforts are generally successful. Great help by the luck of wife. Some girl friend may help in making a rise in life.

(X) Prosperous in life. Does make good progress. Domestic harmony. Comforts of conveyance and living in good houses.

(XI) Makes good gains in life. Likely to prosper in a business concerned with ladies' cosmetics. Some woman may help in establishing some business.

(XII) Heavy expenditure on luxuries. May spend on girl friends. Tactful handling of enemies. Diplomatic.

Positions of Budha in Simha Lagna

House	Effects
(I)	Amasses wealth. Good personality. Practical. Has good source of regular income.
(II)	Happy family life. Business acumen. Earns through commercial intelligence. Possibility of accumulating good wealth in life.
(III)	Commercial insight. Good earning in business. Fortunate. Good relations with relatives.
(IV)	Happy domestic life. Possibility of earning through some business. Facilities of conveyances.
(V)	Very good earning through business transactions. Practical attitude towards life. Girls progeny more in number.
(VI)	Over expenses. Some obstacles in earning. Lives in danger of enemity.
(VII)	Well behaved wife. Good personality. Much earning through partnership. Wife brings luck with her.

(VIII) Happy family life. Good atmosphere in family. Good income. No interest in religious matters.

(IX) An active personality. Betterment through business. Good earning in commercial endeavours.

(X) Facility of conveyances. Good residential facilities. Domestic life happy. Good earning. Successful business career.

(XI) Excellent earning. Successful businessman. Good conversationalist. Helpful friends.

(XII) Expenditure more than the income. Always thinks about increasing income, but remains unsuccessful. No terror of enemies.

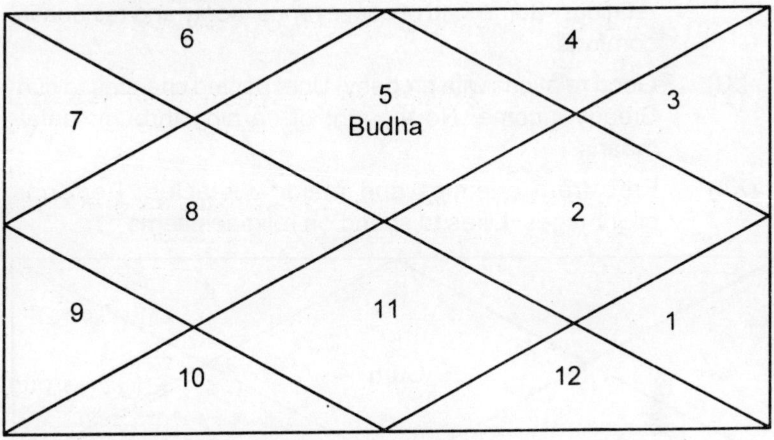

Guru's Positions in the Simha Lagna

House Effects

(I) Very attractive personality. Somewhat corpulent. Obedient and pious wife. Well behaved sons. Fortunate.

(II) Successful career. Free from enemies. Religious temperament. A thirst for spirituality. Happy family.

(III) Lucky. Steady income from any source. Fortunate and good looking wife.

(IV) Some domestic problem. Expenses on religious ceremonies. Likes spiritual pursuits.

(V) Lucky and obedient sons. Slow but steady income. Efforts for betterment rarely go in vain.

(VI) Aims at spiritual emancipation. May settle in some religious place.

(VII) Good personality. Wife charming and well-behaved. A good helpful friendly circle. Steady income.

(VIII) Good longevity. Likes religious pursuits. Possibility of reaching very high stage of spirituality. Expenses on religious performances.

(IX) Gets unexpected rise in life. Sons bring honour. Ethical thinking. Good relation with brothers and sisters.

(X) Very happy family life. Members of the family have cordial relations. Some kind of conveyance facility and residential comforts.

(XI) Good relations with progeny. Unexpected chances to rise. Steady income. No thought of earning through unfair means.

(XII) Free from enemies and major obstacles. Performs pilgrimages. Likes to spend on religious items.

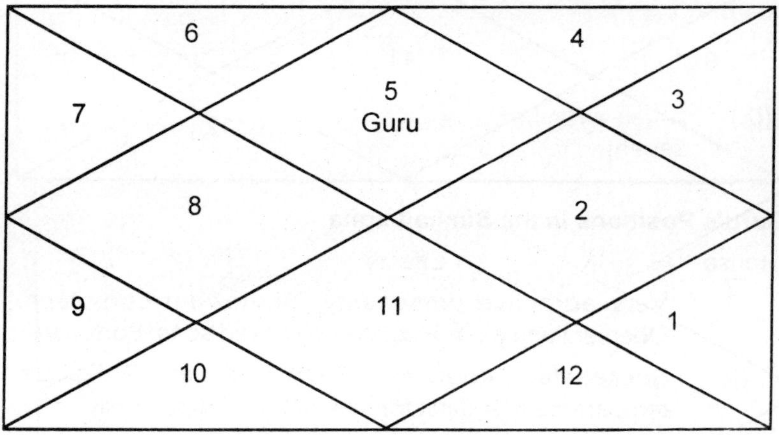

Positions of Shani in Simha Lagna

House	Effects
(I)	Some health problem. Discordant family life. Quarrelsome wife. Problems in career-making.
(II)	Philosophic tendency. Some kind of unhappiness in family. Marriage brings wealth. Wife practical in outlook.
(III)	Very helpful, beautiful and cultured wife. Some problems from progeny. First issue may abort. Some struggle in the initial stages of life.
(IV)	Unhappy domestic life. Dominant and angry wife. Some problems in the place of work. Some health problem.
(V)	Good and helpful wife. Some dissatisfaction from progeny. Marriage brings prosperity. Few friends.
(VI)	Conquers enemies and opposition. Spends money very thoughtfully. Miserly habits.
(VII)	Very wise and thoughtful wife. Some problems of health. Distress from other members of family. Advantages of conveyances.
(VIII)	Very reflective tendency in the field of religion. Hurdles in the making of good career. Some dissatisfaction from members of family.
(IX)	Much struggles in establishing a career. Likely to get repeated failures. No help from wife.

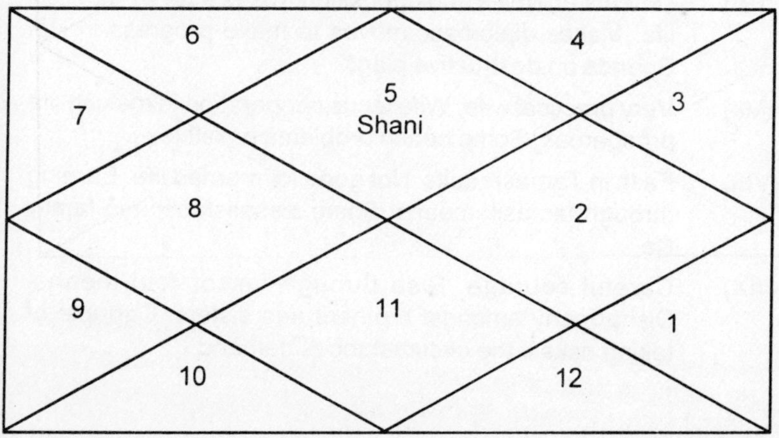

(X) Wife from a rich family. Helpful wife. But some kind of domestic disharmony.

(XI) Much rise after marriage. Wife brings money due to her good luck. Income in the late years of life. Very few but helpful friends.

(XII) Wasteful wife. Expenses more than income. But subjugates enemies and obstacles.

Positions of Rahu in Simha Lagna

House	Effects
(I)	Some problem of health. Possibility of injury of some portion of face or head. Possibility of some surgical treatment. But possibility of success in politics. Works secretly.
(II)	Much money after the age of 42. Some problems in family. Cunning and scheming mind.
(III)	Makes progress through cunning efforts. Very successful in the domain of political life or any business needing such qualification. Disharmony between brothers and sisters.
(IV)	Discontent in family. Possibility of having good immovable property. Has to face intrigues in the place of work.
(V)	First progeny may abort. Cunningness dominates in behaviour. Earns through doubtful means.
(VI)	Defeats enemies and opposition. Rises after 42 years of life. Makes diplomatic moves to make progress in life. Spends on destructive plans.
(VII)	Very practical wife. Wife lends cooperation in making life prosperous. Some health problems possible.
(VIII)	Faith in Tamasik cults. Not good for married life. Earning through tamasik means. Some dissatisfaction in family life.
(IX)	Careful courage. Rise through fair or foul means. Disharmony amongst brothers and sisters. Capable of taking risks if the circumstances demand.

(X)	Good rise after 42 years of age. Political and cunning handlings of situation. Domestic life perturbed. Advantages of good conveyances and residing places.
(XI)	Excellent income. Powerful friends. Good circle. Material affluence.
(XII)	Undue expenses. Spends on Tamasik items. Defeats enemies. Lack of religious tendency.

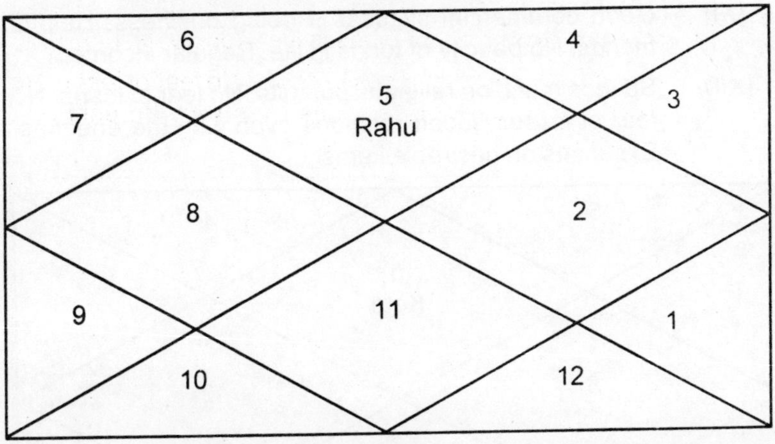

Positions of Ketu in Simha Lagna

House	Effects
(I)	Pleasing personality. Thoughtful temperament. Interested in rational religion. Impressive advancement in life.
(II)	Practical attitude of life. Peaceful family environment. Good balance of money. Inoffensive behaviour.
(III)	Very active. Help from opposite sex in the rise of life. Works smoothly. Good relations with brothers and sisters.
(IV)	Good domestic atmosphere. Contented heart. Advantages of good residences and houses.
(V)	Philanthropic temperament. Thinks about helping others. Smooth sailing with progeny. Religious attitude.
(VI)	Fights bravely against odds and enemies. Victorious in the struggle. Good progress in career.
(VII)	Religious minded and thoughtful wife. Gets affection of wife. Has good rapport with wife and her relatives.

(VIII) Interested in deeper aspect of religion. Happy family environment. Keeps good balance of money.

(IX) Makes good progress in life. Initial struggles, but ultimate victory. Rises to high position in life.

(X) Smooth sailing in the field of activity. Facilities of good residential accommodation and vehicles. May own a good house. Domestic atmosphere calm and quiet.

(XI) Good commercial success if doing business. Helpful friends. No paucity of funds in life. Regular income.

(XII) Spends much on religious pursuits. No fear of loans. No fear of losses. Good relations even with the enemies. Expenses on desirable items.

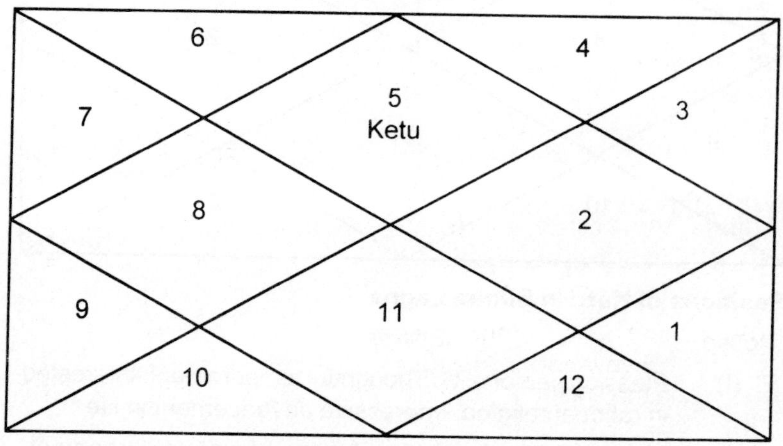

14

KANYA LAGNA

Positions of Surya in Kanya Lagna

House	Effects
(I)	Impressive personality. Habit of over-spending. Hot temperament. Dominating tendency. Wife unhappy because of husband's behaviour.
(II)	Problem of meeting expenses. No interest in conventional religion. Family life not to the expectation.
(III)	Very influential and active. Powerful friends. May get good success if enters politics. A man of courage and confidence.
(IV)	Some discordance in domestic field. Facilities of good conveyances. Majestic living. Accorded respect and awe in the field of work.
(V)	Interest in philosophic matters. Influential friends. First issue may abort. Lack of harmony in relation with progeny.
(VI)	Terror of enemies. Finishes opposition in a ruthless manner. Deep interest in philosophical spheres.
(VII)	Some problems from wife. Wife may be hot tempered. Good personality.
(VIII)	Deep interest in metaphysical pursuits. Possibility of accident. Spends much in charitable works.
(IX)	Makes progress through self-effort. Good relation with brothers. Gets generally success in the efforts made.
(X)	Makes an outstanding progress viewed in the background of one's family. Influential and assertive in the domain of

work. Facilities of vehicles and residential houses. But domestic field lacks satisfaction.

(XI) Expenses more than the income. Influential friends. Can get success if one enters the political life. First child may abort. Earning with honour and principles.

(XII) May visit religious places. May spend on religious rituals. May make rise in some foreign land. A life devoted to religious attainments.

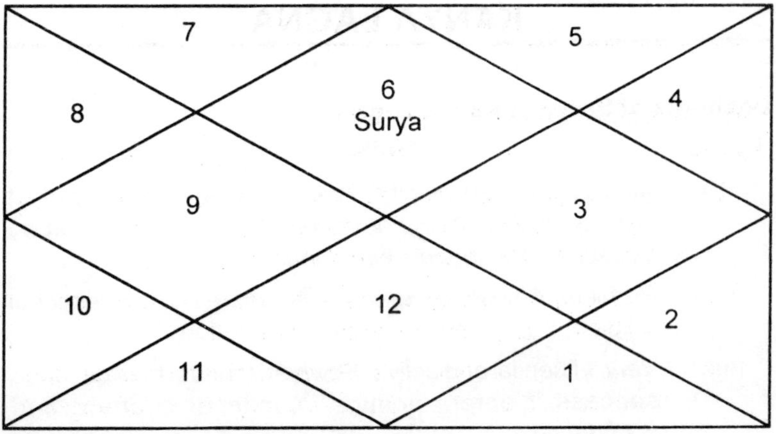

Positions of Chandra in Kanya Lagna

House Effects

(I) Very practical and wise. Good personality. Amiable nature. Wife having pleasing manner. May shine in business field or any other field like computer, moneylending, cooperation, etc.

(II) Good deposits. Harmonious family atmosphere. Astounding success in life. Good conversational ability.

(III) Very active and zestful. Good relations with brothers and sisters. Makes rise in life without much struggle.

(IV) Outstanding success in business or field of profession. Satisfactory domestic conditions. All residential and conveyance facilities.

(V) Commercial outlook of life. Adapt in business matters. Girl progeny may be the first child.

(VI) Some problems in business and occupation. But problems are solved through patience. Health problems may persist for a pretty long period.

(VII) Attractive personality, leaning towards corpulence. Cooperative and wise life partner. Marriage may bring professional progress.

(VIII) Good family environment. Can amass wealth after great struggle. Scant regard for religion. Materialistic attitude.

(IX) Makes great efforts for advancement of career. Not dissuaded by failures. Ultimate success.

(X) Great success in a pursued career. Very practical in business dealings. Can prove a good sales manager. Knows the art of tackling people.

(XI) Commanding position in business circle. Helpful friends. Sometimes business and sometimes it shrinks. But on the whole, prosperity in life.

(XII) Some health problems right from birth. Health problem arises from mental depression. Anxieties concerning profession.

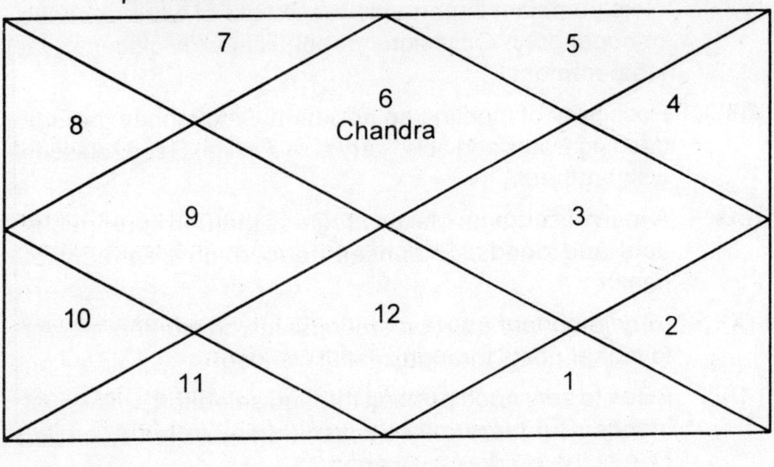

Positions of Mangal in Kanya Lagna

House	Effects
(I)	Possibility of surgical treatment. Hot temperament. Problem of ill health. Dissatisfaction in married life.
(II)	Dissatisfaction in family. Lack of harmony in brothers and sisters. Very active for increasing income. But hurdles in the way. First child may abort.
(III)	Very active. Dashing. Not afraid in taking an initiative. Conflicts in the field of work. Gets importance in the field of work.
(IV)	Dissension in home. Some problems concerning wife. Wife has hot temperament.
(V)	Wife comes from a higher family or status. Efforts are usually rewarded with success. First child may abort. Aggressive thought.
(VI)	Puts down opposition and obstacles. Problem of ill health. Health may need surgical treatment. Dominant position in co-workers.
(VII)	Gets dominant importance in the field of work. A sense of superiority. Occasions of conflicts with officers. Hot temperament.
(VIII)	Possibility of meeting an accident. Gets money through dashing works and acts. Very active in life. Good relations with brothers.
(IX)	A man of courage. Makes progress through courageous acts and deeds. Expenses concerning treatment of health.
(X)	Very important position amongst the co-workers. Rises to higher posts through zestful working.
(XI)	Rises to very good position through self-effort. Influential friends. But there may be disharmony in family circle. One of the children may abort.

(XII) Destroys enemies and opposition. Some wasteful expenses. Worships Kali or Hanuman or any other deity of strength.

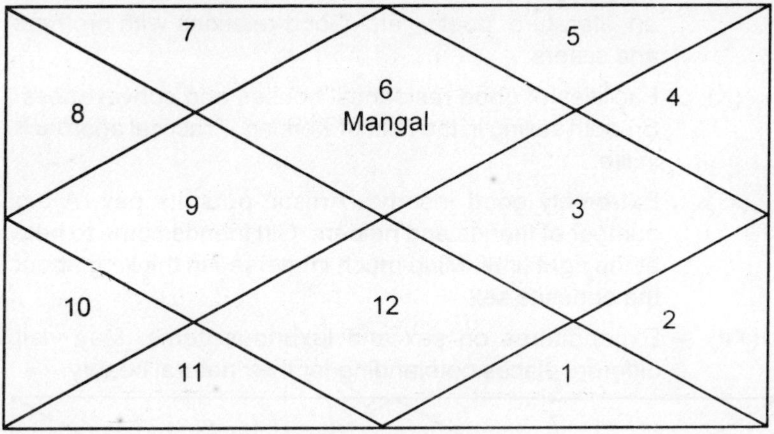

Positions of Shukra in Kanya Lagna

House	Effects
(I)	Handsome personality. Graceful manners. Fortunate. Beautiful wife. Happy family life.
(II)	Beautiful face. Love for fine arts and literature. Good bank balance. Materialistic tendency.
(III)	Fortunate. Early rise in life. May get help from some member of the opposite sex in the advancement of luck. Good relations with brothers and sisters.
(IV)	Harmonious domestic life. Facilities of good residential houses and conveyances. Harmonious environment in the field of working.
(V)	Unexpected chance of advancement. First child may be a girl. Good relations with children. Good flow of income.
(VI)	Some hurdles in the furthering of career. Expenses on luxuries. Expenses on artistic or literary projects.
(VII)	Noteworthy progress in life. A member of opposite sex plays an important role in the rise. Artistic talent. Very beautiful wife. Good personality.

(VIII) Attractive face. Good bank balance. Materialistic tendency. Harmony in family. Sweet way of talking.

(IX) Very good rise in life. Progress may be in the domain of art, literature, poetry, etc. Good relations with brothers and sisters.

(X) Facilities of good residential houses and conveyances. Smooth sailing in the field of working. Practical approach in life.

(XI) Extremely good income. Artistic pursuits pay. A big number of friends.and helpers. Girl friends come to help at the right time. Mind much immersed in thinking about the opposite sex.

(XII) Expenditures on sex and luxurious items. May visit different places outstanding for their natural beauty.

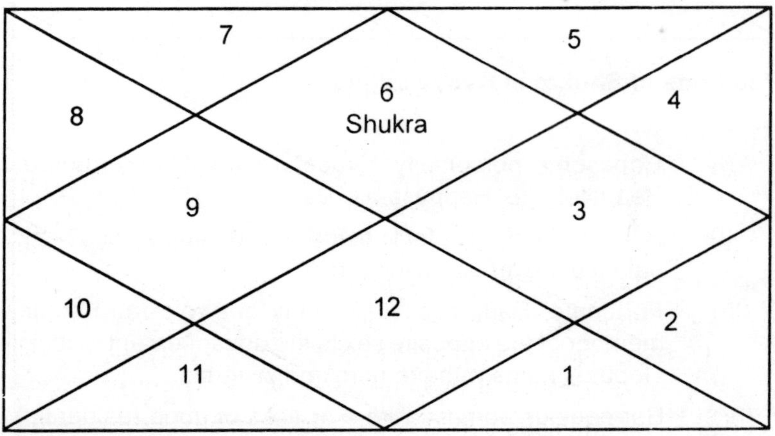

Positions of Budha in Kanya Lagna

House Effects

(I) Extremely practical and empirical in behaviour. Good personality. Remarkable rise in life. Good wife. Can prove to be a very big businessman. Wise and intelligent.

(II) Very wealthy. Good family environment. Materialistic outlook. Early rise in life.

(III) Good relations with brothers and sisters. Very active and successful in life.

(IV) Makes an outstanding progress in life. All facilities of residential houses and conveyances.

(V) Unexpected opportunities of progress in life. Helpful children. Number of girl child more than the number of male children. Practical thinking and conduct.

(VI) Hurdles in career making. Gets out of the difficulties through patience and calculated moves.

(VII) There may be slight health problems. Practical wife. Should avoid partnerships in business. Good personality.

(VIII) Some setbacks in business and career. Hardships in getting wealth. But good environment in family.

(IX) Very active. Has much success in attempted moves. Good relations with relatives.

(X) Outstanding progress in career. Practical, successful, intelligent, reputed.

(XI) Mind always busy in planning for success in a career. Wise and intelligent. Gets good success after the age of 32. Can adjust with every type of person.

(XII) Very intelligent planner. Has courage to spend one's plan. Gets success despite competition and opposition.

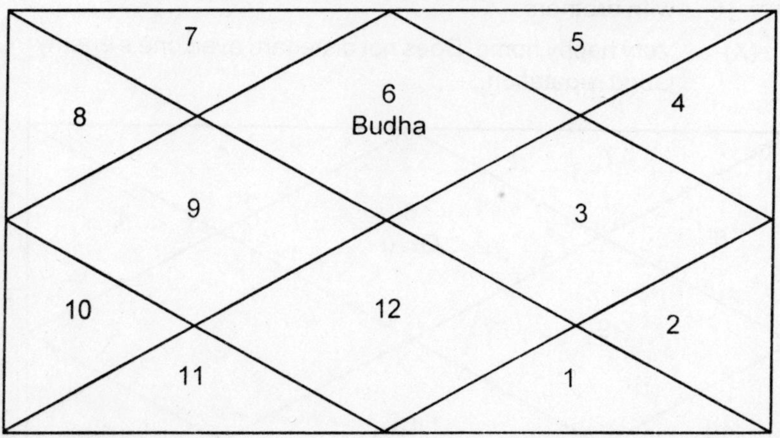

Guru in Kanya Lagna— Different Positions

House	Effects
(I)	Good personality. Religious minded wife. Happy home. Good children. Number of sons may be more than that of daughters. Makes slow but steady progress in life.
(II)	Marriage brings luck. Steady income. Religious tendency. Happy home. Good education.
(III)	Good relations with brothers. Steady income. Good relations with wife. Fortunate. May get a good start in the early years of life.
(IV)	Good domestic life. But possibility of some discontent. Spending on religious items. May perform pilgrimages.
(V)	Good income. May settle in life quite early. Helpful friends.
(VI)	Tries to settle dispute through mutual agreement. Spends on religious obligations.
(VII)	Very helpful wife. Good personality. Good relations with brothers, steady income.
(VIII)	A long life. Deeply religious nature. Gets good help from friends.
(IX)	Bright children get settled in life quite early. Good relations with brothers.
(X)	Very happy home. Does not disregard even one's enemy. Good reputation.

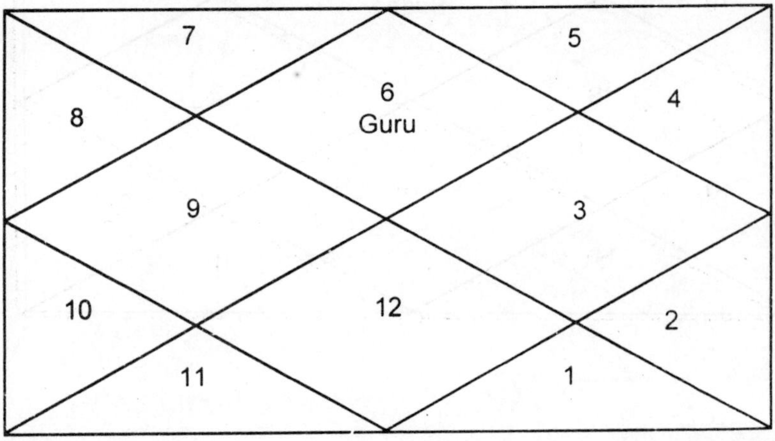

(XI) Very helpful friends. Very active nature. Good relations with brothers.

(XII) Takes deep interest in religious matters. Tries to implement religious principles in life. Performs religious rites. Visits religious places.

Positions of Shani in Kanya Lagna

House	Effects
(I)	Good personality. Beautiful but non-cooperative wife. Struggles in life. May be betrayed by any woman. Lacks artistic tendency.
(II)	Windfall of money sometime in life. Progeny brings luck and money. There may be slight dissatisfaction in the family. Some sort of philosophical leaning.
(III)	Opposition from progeny. Non-harmonious relations with brothers and sisters. Hurdles to be crossed in shaping a fine career. Very active, but efforts fail most of the time.
(IV)	Some discontents in domestic field. Facilities of residential houses and conveyances lacking. Opposition and conflict in the place of working.
(V)	There may be slight difference of opinion with progeny. But the latter makes good progress and brings respect to parents. Discontent from wife. Income not to one's satisfaction or comes rather late in life.
(VI)	Victorious over foes and opposition of any kind. Spends money carefully. Miserly habits. A man of depth and not show.
(VII)	Adjustment with wife with difficulty. Non-attractive looks. Hurdles in progress. Dissatisfaction on the home front.
(VIII)	Discontent in family. Wealth amassed in later life, after a great effort and long struggle. Outspoken by nature.
(IX)	Unexpected rise after thirty-six years of age. Not overcome by failures. Income comes after great labour. Not very cordial relations with brothers and sisters.
(X)	Makes progress rather late in life. Some troubles in the domestic sphere. Not very cordial relations with wife. Keeps watch on expenses.

(XI) Non-steady income. But unexpected chances in life for betterment and income. Friends few but reliable. Some kind of health problem.

(XII) Overcome opposition and enemies. Frugal habits. A tendency of deep thinking. Non-conventional attitude in religion. Amasses wealth through some unexpected chances or efforts of progeny.

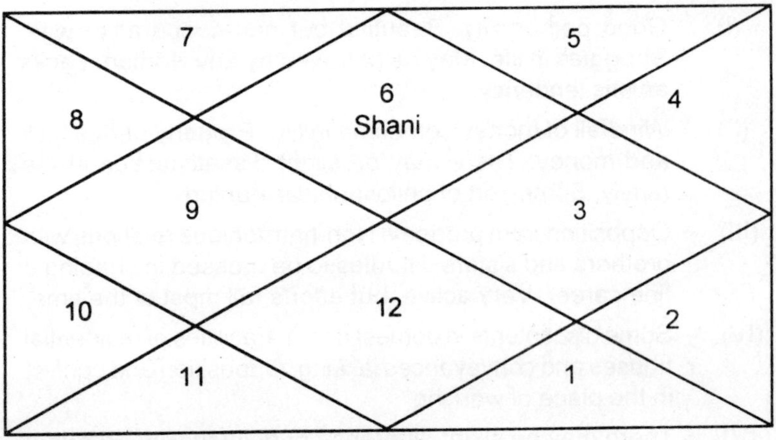

Positions of Rahu in Kanya Lagna

House	Effects
(I)	Some scar on the face. Cunning and practical. Can be successful in politics and business needing cunningness. Some problems from wife. Good rise in life after the age of 42.
(II)	Crafty speech. Some problems from family. But diplomatic in speech and behaviour. Can earn much through fair or foul means. No interest in simple religion.
(III)	Very active and diplomatic. Dashing. Uncordial relations with brothers and sisters. Can stoop to any level for getting things done.
(IV)	Unhappy domestic life. But facilities of conveyances and residential houses. Hurdles in education.
(V)	First progeny may abort. Progeny makes progress in life. But relations not cordial. Very practical intelligence.

(VI) Puts down opposition and competition. Wins through careful planning.

(VII) Problems in marriage. No cordial relations between husband and wife. Some problems of health.

(VIII) Faith in Tamasik religion or Tantrik practices. Possibility of accident. Amasses wealth through malpractices.

(IX) Great progress in material direction. Goes forward despite hurdles. Uncordial relations with brothers and sisters.

(X) Outstanding progress in practical life. May get success in political life. Facilities of residence and conveyances.

(XI) Mental tarment due to negative thinking. Friends belonging to a scheming nature lost or unreliable.

(XII) Can meet any opposition or competition. Expenditure in destructive planning.

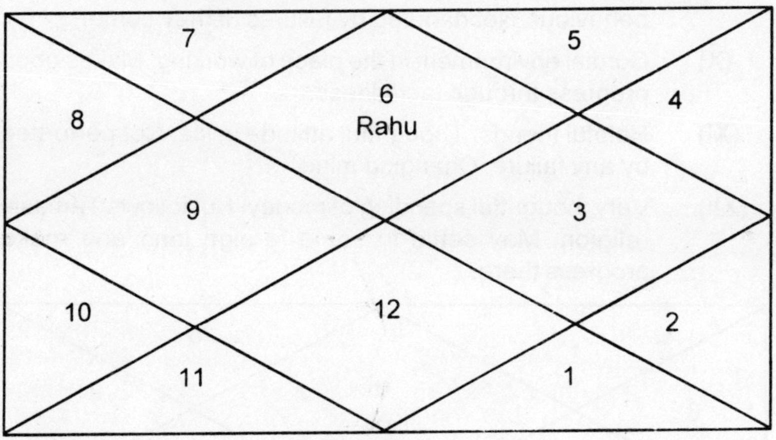

Positions of Ketu in Kanya Lagna

House Effects

(I) Good personality. Practical attitude. Intelligent. Makes progress through constructive ways and right planning. Makes good progress after 46 years of age.

(II) Amasses huge wealth. Good relations with members of family. Speech liked by all.

(III) Very active. Does not sit idle. Believes in making one's career through self-effort. Good relations with brothers and sisters.

(IV) Some problems in domestic field. All facilities of conveyance and material affluence available.

(V) Very intelligent and thoughtful. Cooperative progeny. Very refined manners.

(VI) Overcomes enemies and hurdles in a thoughtful manner. Never loses poise of mind.

(VII) Intelligent and cooperative wife. Threat in partnership. May get good support from wife's parents.

(VIII) Faith in devilish religion. But thoughtful and practical. Amasses wealth. Good relations with members of family.

(IX) Makes great progress through self-effort. Graceful in behaviour. Not danuted by failures, if they come.

(X) Cordial environment in the place of working. Makes good progress through tactfulness.

(XI) Helpful friends. Thoughtful attitude in life. Not perturbed by any failure. Changing mind.

(XII) Very thoughtful spending of money. But follows Tamasik religion. May settle in some foreign land and make progress there.

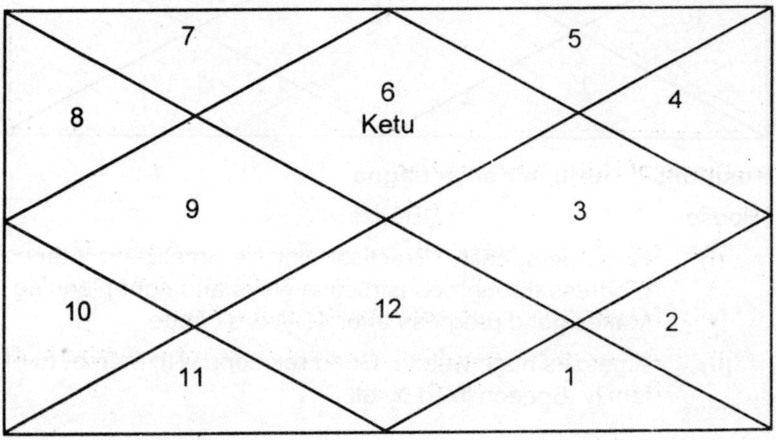

15

TULA LAGNA

Positions of Surya in Tula Lagna

House	Effects
(I)	Difficulty in earning sufficient money. Hot temperament. Dissatisfaction from wife. Impressive personality. Tense relations with officers. Unreliable friends.
(II)	Huge earnings. Happy family. Good learning. Good relations with political leaders. Good relations with officers.
(III)	Very active and successful. Dashing. Advancement of fortune with the help of political leaders of superior authorities.
(IV)	Domestic problems. Facilities of conveyances. Uneasy relations with mother or lacks mothers favour.
(V)	Gets unexpected chances of progress. Good help and cooperation from friends. Friends are important persons and possess commanding positions.
(VI)	Conquers enemies and oppositions. Generally good health. Friends may fail when their cooperation is needed.
(VII)	Significant position attained through the help of very influential friends. Huge earnings. But some problems concerning wife possible. Hot temperament. Aristocratic habits.
(VIII)	Possibility of some accident. Interest in metaphysical subjects. May make progress in the direction of seeking truth about the soul.

(IX) Makes outstanding progress through the help of important friends. Good income. General success. Lover of learning.

(X) Holds outstanding position in the field of working. Some domestic problems possible. Facilities of conveyance and residential places. Egoistic temperament.

(XI) Outstanding income. May get top position in the domain of political career. Commands wide popularity and respect.

(XII) Destroys opposition and enemies. Exorbitant expenses. Lives a life of magnificence.

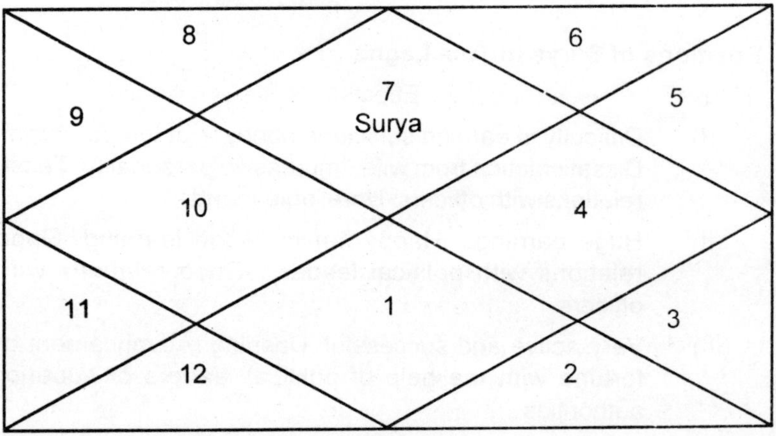

Positions of Chandra in Tula Lagna

House	Effects
(I)	A lover of art and music. Lover of justice and fair play. Impartial. Lovable nature. Popular amongst ladies.
(II)	Hot temperament. Earns through courageous acts. Happiness of family. Loves martial arts.
(III)	Religious temperament. Attains position through righteous acts. Good relations with brothers and sisters.
(IV)	Domestic peace. Facilities of conveyances. Popular amongst colleagues. Peaceful life.
(V)	Thoughtful temperament. First issue may be a girl. Helpful friends. Positive thinking.

(VI) Obstacles in progress. But they disappear in course of time. Friends help when their help is needed.

(VII) Obstinate. A man of determination. Beautiful wife. Becomes popular due to fair and free acts.

(VIII) A man of devotion. Family cooperative. Lover of religious practices. Makes progress despite hurdles.

(IX) Very practical and adjusting. Learned. Thoughtful. Makes any attempt after cool consideration of the outcome. Progress after the age of 32.

(X) A man of many thoughts. Many plannings for life. Career full of changes. But every change brings higher positions. A person loved by everybody due to his amiable nature.

(XI) A great push in a career due to the help of friends who enjoy commanding positions. A man of strict principles. Friends few but have commanding authority.

(XII) Many obstacles in life. But they disappear in course of time. Expenditure on religious items. Believes in simple religion.

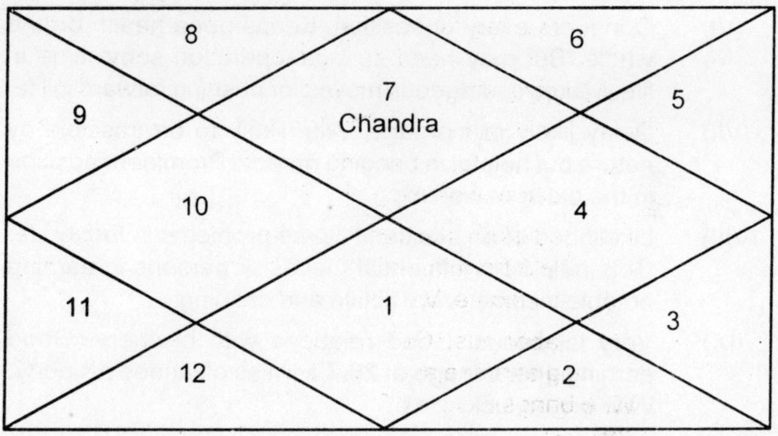

Positions of Mangal in Tula Lagna

House	Effects
(I)	Wife is likely to have hot temperament. Delay in marriage. Some health problems possible. Good earning. Courageous. Dominating nature.
(II)	Amasses huge amount of money. Marriage brings luck and position. Good education. Makes progress through struggle and conflicts.
(III)	Very active. Moneyed. Holds prominent position in the field of activity. Good relations with brothers and sisters. Puts down opposition and disagreements.
(IV)	Wife comes from a higher strata of society. Her nature is likely to be dominating. Marriage brings good luck and status. Rises to responsible positions in service or the field of work.
(V)	First child may abort. Somewhat tense relation with progeny. Good earning through influential friends. Loves to be friend important persons.
(VI)	Conquers every opposition. Keeps good health on the whole. But may need surgical operation some time in life. Makes courageous moves for pushing forward in life.
(VII)	Delay likely in marriage. Wife likely to be irascible by nature but helpful in bringing money. Prominent position in the place of working.
(VIII)	Likelihood of an accident. Some problems in family life. Gets help from influential friends or persons in earning notable income. Very active and dashing.
(IX)	Very laborious. Good relations with brothers. Good earning after the age of 28. Facilities of landed property. Wife brings luck.
(X)	Full of self-confidence. Somewhat hot temperament. Earns good landed property. First issue may abort. May need some kind of surgical operation for treatment some time in life.
(XI)	Very good earning through influential friends. May get very significant position in political life. May not have smooth relations.

(XII) Spending habit. Required to spend on litigation. Not happy with the behaviour of wife. Comes out successful from every struggle and opposition.

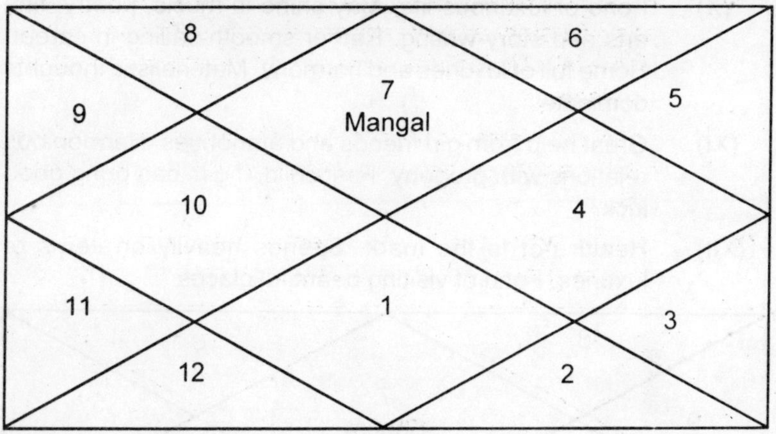

Positions of Shukra in Tula Lagna

House	Effects
(I)	Handsome personality. Lover of fine arts like music, painting, poetry, etc., Popularity amongst ladies. Good looking wife.
(II)	Happy family life. Cooperative members of family. Sweet speech. Not popular amongst ladies.
(III)	Active. Help from a member of opposite sex. Smooth sailing in life. Makes good progress in career.
(IV)	Facilities of conveyance, residential houses and luxuries. Domestic life full of peace and glitter. Easy success in the field of working.
(V)	Gets a very good unexpected opportunities in life for advancement. Diplomatic, may get some help from a girl friend. First issue is likely to be a girl.
(VI)	Some problems about health. But overcomes diseases and oppositions gracefully. Expenses on luxury items.
(VII)	Good-looking wife. But she may be rather quarrelsome. Good personality. Fond of good dresses.
(VIII)	Materialistic attitude. Health problems. Happy family life. May accumulate money in course of time.

(IX) Very good successes in life. Great push toward betterment from the age of 32. Success may be achieved in the early twenties.

(X) Fond of luxurious life. May shine in music, poetry, fine arts and story-writing. Rather smooth sailing in career. Home full of luxuries and harmony. Materialistic thoughts dominate.

(XI) Great help from girl friends and authorities. Harmonious relations with progeny. First child, if girl, can bring good luck.

(XII) Health not to the mark. Spends heavily on items of luxuries. Fond of visiting beautiful places.

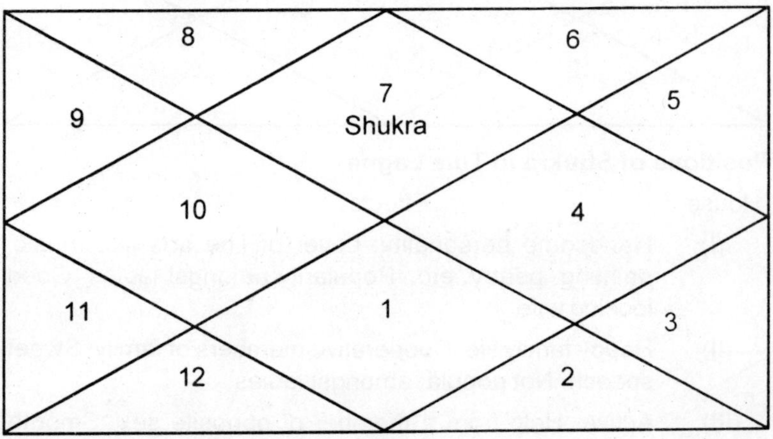

Positions of Budha in Tula Lagna

House Effects

(I) Expenses more than the income. Wise and practical. Good personality. Makes a good rise in life through implementation of well-considered plans.

(II) Happy family life. Love for learning. Earns much through business and efforts. Has good relations with the relatives.

(III) Active. Help from a member of opposite sex. Smooth sailing in life. Makes good progress in career.

(IV) Facilities of conveyances and residential houses. Has good relations with mother. Makes progress in career through patience and planning.

(V) Gets many unexpected chances for the furtherance of career. Earns much through cooperation of influential friends. First issue may be a girl.

(VI) Faces many hurdles in life. Practical attitude becomes helpful. Control on expenses.

(VII) Helping and cooperative wife who gives practical suggestions.

(VIII) Good family life. Harmony prevails. No interest in real religion in reality.

(IX) Good rise after the age of 32. Makes steady progress. Capacity of adjustment. Can pull on well with all types of persons.

(X) Some problems in career. But a methodical approach helps in carving out good future. Good relation with brothers and sisters.

(XI) Huge earning possible. Sterling help from friends. Harmonious relations with all.

(XII) Expensive planning. Spends money after a cool consideration of all factors. May settle away from the birth-place.

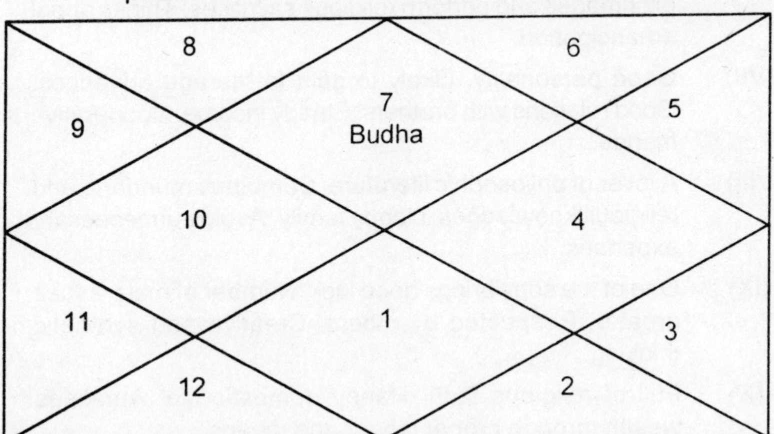

Positions of Guru in Tula Lagna

House	Effects
(I)	Ill health. Good personality. Beautiful and obedient wife. Number of male issues more than the female issues. First child is likely to be a son.
(II)	A love for philosophical thinking. Atmosphere in family is likely to be religious. Popularity and success in the field of activity.
(III)	Very active and popular. Income steady. A circle of important position-holders. May get good help from friends.
(IV)	Some problems on the home front. But good and helpful atmosphere in the field of working. Undertakes many journeys to holy places. Likes to spend on religious occasions.
(V)	Creative thinking. Gets good chance for betterment of career. Chance may come at about 16 years age. Ample cooperation from influential friends.
(VI)	Accumulates wealth. Religious and God-fearing family. Expenses on legitimate grounds. May undertake pilgrimages and perform religious sacrifices. Thinks about emancipation.
(VII)	Good personality. Likely to gain fat as age advances. Good relations with brothers. Steady income. Cooperative friends.
(VIII)	A lover of philosophic literature. Combines mundane and religious knowledges. Happy family. Avoids unnecessary expenses.
(IX)	One of the sons brings good luck. Number of male issues greater. Respected by others. Creative and synthetic thinking.
(X)	Full of religious faith. Happy domestic life. Amasses wealth through proper labour and means.
(XI)	Excellent response from friends. Efforts get rewarded. Good relations with members of family.

(XII)	Undertake many journeys to places of religious significance. Tries for getting liberation. May get some gift from father. A person having no enemies.

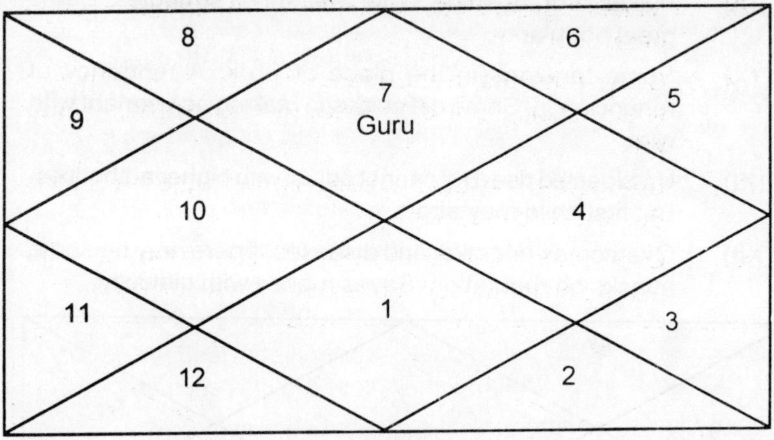

Positions of Shani in Tula Lagna

House	Effects
(I)	A grand rise in life in an unexpected way. One of the progeney brings good laurels. Some problem from wife. Very active and successful.
(II)	Members of family do not cooperate. But earns good property and conveyances. May not be liked much by the mother.
(III)	Very active and gets unexpected chances of progress in life. Speech rather hard. Good knowledge of metaphysical topics.
(IV)	May not get mother's protection for long time. But her affection is supreme. Good domestic facilities. Makes a push for a higher position after 36 years of age.
(V)	First issue may abort. Man of few words but great deeds. Intelligent and reliable. Popular.
(VI)	Not afraid of enemies and opposition. Spends money very carefully. Always active.
(VII)	May lack handsome personality. Has to face struggles and conflict for progress. But ultimately successful.

(VIII) Good longevity. Some hurdles in work. Saves money with difficulty. A love for philosophical lore.

(IX) Makes a great stride in life after initial struggles. Earns great popularity.

(X) Some tensions in the place of work. A tendency of renunciation. Some difficulties in making adjustment with wife.

(XI) Unexpected rise. But cannot adjust with higher authorities. But first child may abort.

(XII) Overcomes enemies and diseases. There may be some attacks on reputation. Saves money with difficulty.

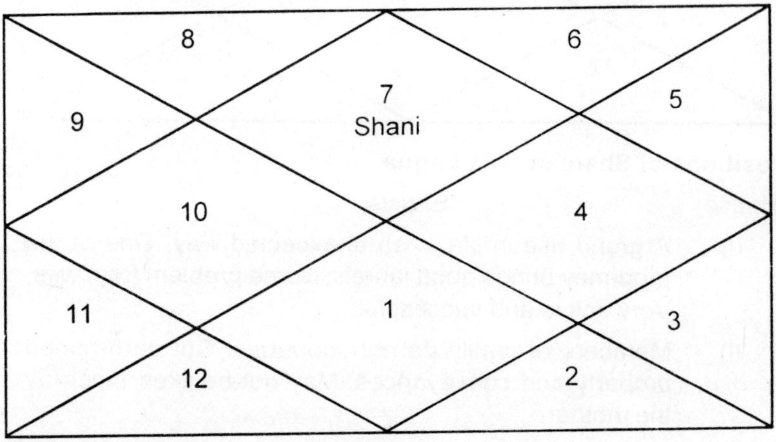

Positions of Rahu in Tula Lagna

House Effects

(I) Handsome personality. Diplomatic nature. Some surgical treatment. Some problems concerning marriage settlement.

(II) Some problems concerning family. Earns money through bold acts. Unpleasant speech.

(III) Very active. Believes in getting things done through fair or foul means. Gets success through cunning acts.

(IV) Some domestic problems. Gets facilities of conveyances and residence. Practical outlook. May not have very pleasant relations with mother.

(V) Manoeuvring intelligence. First child may abort. Some tensions from children. Grasps every opportunity for betterment.

(VI) Overcomes diseases and opposition. Spends money on destructive items. Capacity of manipulating the things.

(VII) Problems in settling marriage. Non-smooth relations with wife. Quarrelsome wife.

(VIII) Possibility of an accident. Faith in Tamasik religion. Accumulates money through unfair means.

(IX) Makes good rise in life after the age of 42. Capable of making life prosperous through any means. May be cheated at times.

(X) Tamasik way of acting. Can rise in life through unfair means. Restless mind.

(XI) Can get success in political field. Can earn through skilful planning. Friendship with unsocial elements.

(XII) Can settle outside one's land. Prospers in a foreign nation. Fond of touring foreign countries. Expenses on unproductive items.

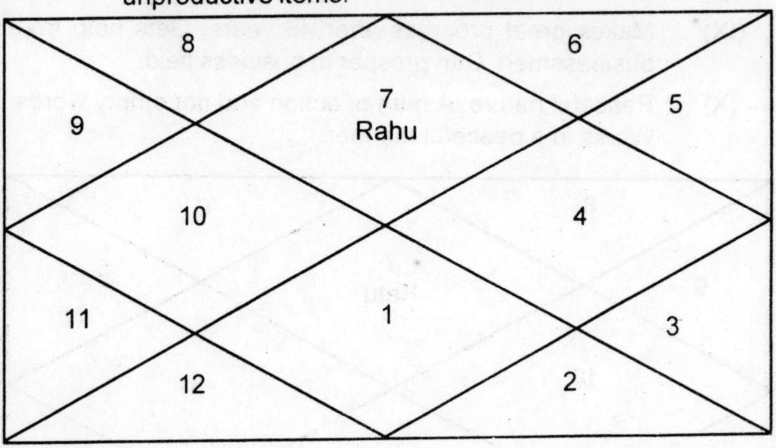

Positions of Ketu in Tula Lagna

House	Effects
(I)	Thoughtful nature. Capacity of adjusting anywhere and at any period. Body may lack handsomeness.
(II)	Earns money through thoughtful ways. Good education. Family environment harmonious. Courageous.
(III)	Very active. Thoughtful. Gets good success after 46. Good relations with brothers.
(IV)	Good family environment. Facilities of conveyances. Prosperous family.
(V)	Creative intelligence. Gets good opportunities in life. Helpful friends. Thoughtful nature.
(VI)	Overcomes enemies through patience and intelligence. Believes in Rajasik religion.
(VII)	Intelligent wife. Wife cooperates in life. Dashing nature. Success through partnership in business.
(VIII)	Religious fanaticism. Accumulates money. Soft speech. Harmonious environment in family.
(IX)	Makes great progress after 46 years. Gets help from businessmen. Can prosper in business field.
(X)	Peaceful nature. A man of action and not empty words. Works in a peaceful manner.

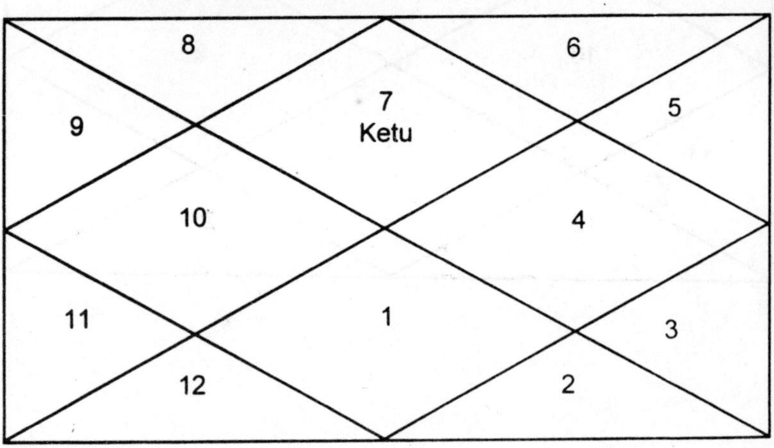

(XI) Influential friends. Gets their full cooperation, extraordinary money and fame.

(XII) May settle in a foreign land. Spends money in a thoughtful way. Believes in making charities and helping others through money.

16

VRISHCHIK LAGNA

Positions of Surya in the Vrishchik Lagna

House	Effects
(I)	Majestic personality. Courageous, confident, occupies a position of importance and emenence.
(II)	Good earning and saving. Religious temperament. Good family. Higher education. Man of words.
(III)	Very active and successful. Helped by important persons in the betterment of the career.
(IV)	Some domestic problems. Does not pull well with mother. Occupies good position in the field of work. Respected by people.
(V)	First child may abort. Cooperative nature. Eminent. Constructive thinking. Enjoys the company of prominent friends.
(VI)	Crushes enemies. Rises to the top position in the field of working despite odds.
(VII)	Wife may not be very cooperative. Problems in adjusting with wife. Wife may be boastful.Good personality.
(VIII)	Possibility of some accident. Good family life. Good education. Loves metaphysical musings.
(IX)	Pushes forward in life by dint of one's boldness and courage. May nurse a sense of pride.
(X)	Rises to top position in life. Enjoys good reputation. A man of principles. Full of self-confidence. Enjoys facilities of conveyances and good residence.

(XI) Helped by friends. Has a prominent position in one's group of friends. Gets good opportunities to rise in life in an unexpected manner.

(XII) Many conflicts in the field of working. Expenses on wasteful items. May fall from a position of importance.

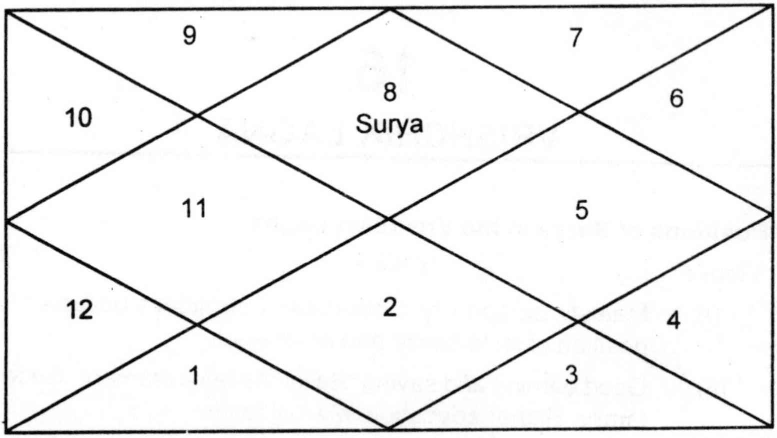

Positions of Chandra in Vrishchik Lagna

House	Effects
(I)	Obstacles in the path of progress. Pessimistic attitude. Handsome personality. Wife pretty. Irascible temperament.
(II)	Very good atmosphere in family. Religious temperament. Good saving. Does not compromise on principles.
(III)	Active. Early rise in life. Fortunate. May be helped by any lady in the betterment of fortune.
(IV)	Happy domestic life. Facilities of conveyances and residential conveniences. Good environment in the place of working.
(V)	Gets unexpected fine opportunities for betterment. Children obedient and prosperous. Believes in living morally elevated life.
(VI)	Brave. Struggles in the initial stages of life. But ultimate victory over obstacles. Journeys to the holy places.

(VII) Settles in life in the early twenties of life. Cheerful temperament. But holds strong views. Pretty wife. Good personality.

(VIII) Struggles in the beginning of life. Religious faith. Good and adjusting wife. Good savings in life.

(IX) Settles in life quite early. Smooth sailing in life. Greeted by successes generally.

(X) Courageous and bold. Full of confidence. Aggressive does not make any compromise on principles. Happy domestic life. Home full of sufficient facilities.

(XI) Practical. Business-minded. Children well-behaved and fortunate. Good unexpected chances in life. Ability to adapt.

(XII) Adjusting nature. Lover of justice. Faces hurdles in the betterment of life. But ultimate victory over all the obstacles. Liked by people.

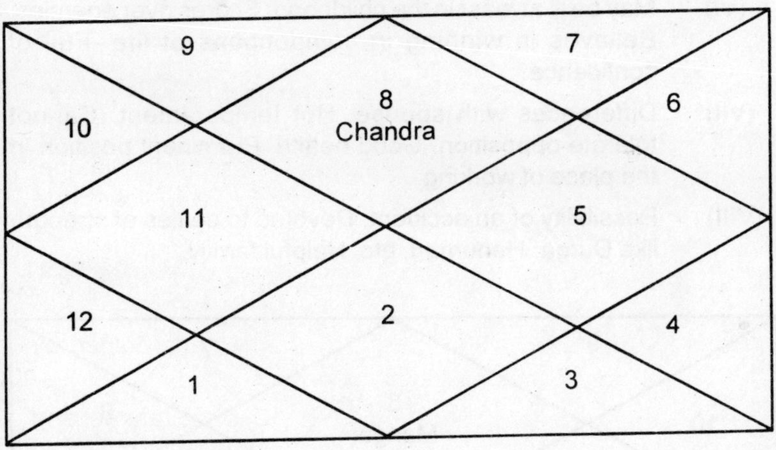

Mangal's Positions in the Vrishchik Lagna

House	Effects
(I)	Good health, very courageous. Hot temperament. Strict disciplinarian. Lover of martial arts. Lover of outdoor games. May not pull well with wife.
(II)	Happiness from family. Good education. Outspoken. First child may abort. Male children more than the female ones.
(III)	Excellent health. Creates enemies but crushes them if they come in opposition. Makes a head way in life by conquering difficulties.
(IV)	Some domestic problems. Recipient of chattel property. Differences with wife and partners. Wields authority in the place of working.
(V)	Possibility of abortion of a child. Differences with children. Holds dominant position amongst friends.
(VI)	May be ill at least in the childhood. Scores over enemies. Believes in winning in competitions of life. Full of confidence.
(VII)	Differences with spouse. Hot temperament. Cannot tolerate opposition. Good health. Prominent position in the place of working.
(VIII)	Possibility of an accident. Devoted to deities of strength like Durga, Hanuman, etc. Helpful family.

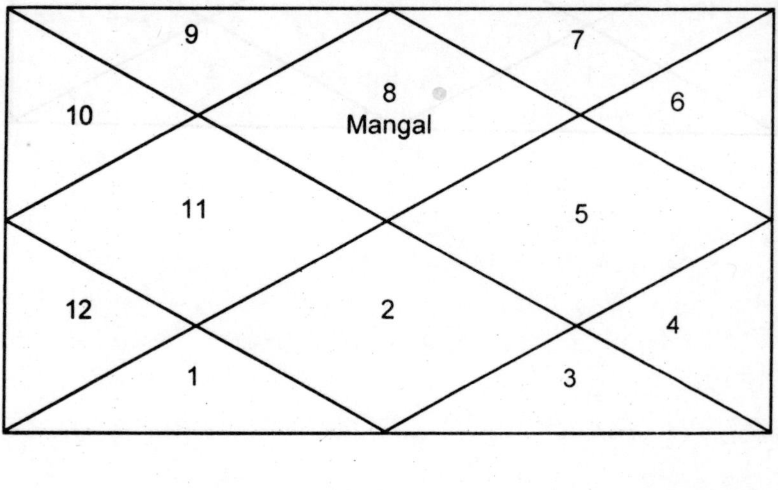

(IX) Irascible. Speaks loudly but lacks courage. Cannot pull well with brothers.

(X) Rises to very prominent position in life. Very good health and position. Possibility of an abortion of a child. All domestic facilities available.

(XI) Saves much through doing daring acts. Some differences with children. One child may abort.

(XII) Wasteful expenses. Loves picking strife and conquering opposition. Very active. But some problem of health may be present.

Shukra's Positions in Vrishchik Lagna

House	Effects
(I)	Charming wife. Expensive habits. Love for arts. Cannot have very smooth relations with a member of opposite sex.
(II)	Expenses more than the income. Calm on the family front. Sweet tongued. Wife cooperative. Marriage brings good luck.
(III)	Good relations with brothers and sisters. Early rise in life. Loved by the members of opposite sex.
(IV)	Luxuries of life. Facilities of conveyance and residence. No serious domestic problem. Pulls on well in the place of work. Diplomatic approach in dealing with others.
(V)	Beautiful and intelligent wife. Marriage brings prosperity. Popular amongst friends. Number of female issues more than that of male issues.
(VI)	Spends heavily on luxuries. Wife has non-adjusting nature. Marriage does not bring peace.
(VII)	Very sensible and charming wife. Can have good adjustment with partners. Handsome personality.
(VIII)	Happy married life. Peaceful family environment. Good education. Hedonistic philosophy of life.
(IX)	Early rise in life. Career receives a help from a member of opposite sex. Good relations with brothers and sisters. Very active.

(X) Happy domestic life. Facilities of conveyances and residences. Good motherly affection. Some lady holding authority may give help in advancing career.

(XI) Practical wife. Marriage brings prosperity and income. Good help from friends. But expensive habits.

(XII) Revels in spending on luxuries. Tactful handling of the enemies. Accepts a philosophy of materialism. May prosper in a foreign land.

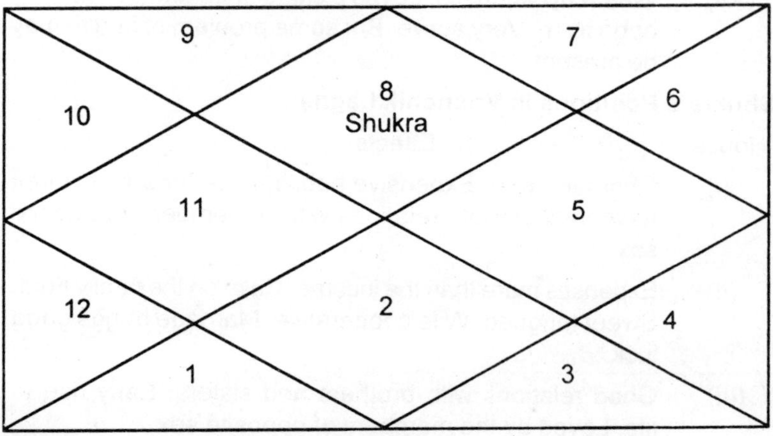

Positions of Budha in Vrishchik Lagna

House	Effects
(I)	Very good earning. Good personality. Practical. Very fortunate from the standpoint of money and friendship. Adjusting wife.
(II)	Very good saving. Happy family life. Educated. Good conversationalist. Practical in dealing with others.
(III)	Very active. Makes rapid progress after the age of 32. A great planner.
(IV)	Happy domestic environment. Makes progress through practical conduct. Gets popularity as a successful dealer.
(V)	Helped by friends. But some friends may try to spoil the career. Non-satisfactory behaviour of children. Practical outlook of life.

(VI) Has to face enemies and difficulties in life for progress. Has to spend on litigation.

(VII) Practical wife. Marriage may bring success in course of time. Good personality. Gets popularity as a practical person.

(VIII) Happy family life. Good education. Good savings. Scant faith in religion.

(IX) Many imaginary plans for future. Gets good success after 32 years of age. May prosper in some business.

(X) Can take risks in business. Can befriend persons of authority. Being practical, tries to gather all the domestic facilities. Good education.

(XI) Extraordinary income in the context of home environment. Very practical in commerce. Gets good cooperation from friends. May prove to be a good conversationalist or speaker.

(XII) Heavy expenses. Friends may bring losses. May come to grief because of wrong planning.

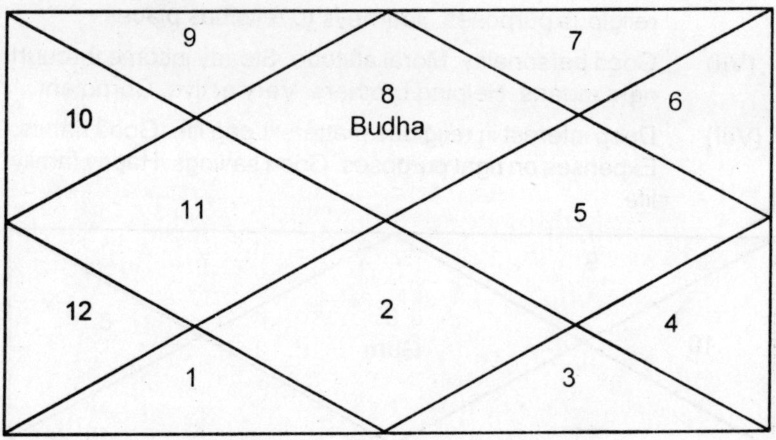

Positions of Guru in Vrishchik Lagna

House	Effects
(I)	Gets good chance of betterment in an unexpected manner. May get a very lasting reputation. Blessed with sons. Fortunate. Good personality leaning towards heftiness. Religious-minded wife.
(II)	Very good saving in life. Money earned through pious means. Happy married life. Leaning of religious nature. Faith in God and traditions.
(III)	Settles in life quite early. Helped by faith in God. Steady income. Religious-minded wife.
(IV)	Happy domestic life. But some kind of dissatisfaction may be present. Journeys to holy places. Love for religion and philosophy.
(V)	Gets good chance in an unexpected manner. Gets good reputation in an unexpected way. Helping friends. Steady income. Good health.
(VI)	Some problems concerning progeny. Expenses on religious purposes. Journeys to religious places.
(VII)	Good personality. Moral attitude. Steady income through right means. Helping brothers. Very active. Corpolent.
(VIII)	Deep interest in religious matters. Long life. Good habits. Expenses on right purposes. Good savings. Happy family life.

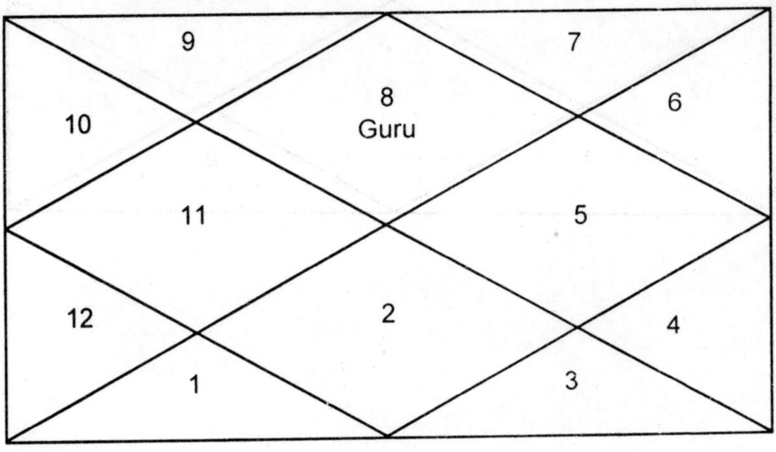

(IX) Settles in life very early. Gets unexpected chances for progress in life. Earns good reputation. Blessed with sons. Moral attitude.

(X) Domestic bliss. Home atmosphere peaceful. Contented life. Loving mother.

(XI) Good sons. Help from sons. Sons bring reputation and popularity. Gets money through religious writing or teaching. Obedient wife.

(XII) Tries to get emancipation. Devoted to religious matters. Fondness for making religious journeys and giving reasonable charities. Long life. Contented home.

Positions of Shani in Vrishchik Lagna

House	Effects
(I)	Some struggles in domestic life. Does not get enough cooperation from brothers. Some hindrances in the place of working. Some differences of opinion with wife.
(II)	Outspoken. Some difficulties in family. Financial miseries. But things improve in later years of age.
(III)	Very active. Good cooperation from brothers. First child may abort. Victories over obstacles. Has to settle in life after much struggle.
(IV)	Initial difficulties on home front. May not get parental affection. Minor health problems. Affluent conditions of home in later life.
(V)	Some differences with wife or late marriage. Gains popularity through good works. Amasses wealth in later life.
(VI)	Initial struggles. But later successes. Mind given to metaphysical thought. Spends money on reasonable grounds alone.
(VII)	Not very beautiful personality. But home front prosperous. Moves forward through struggles and impediments.
(VIII)	Good longevity. Family has to struggle. Outspoken. Conflicts with authorities in the place of working. Follows rational religion.

(IX) Thoughtful nature. Good relations with brothers. Has to face impediments in the path of progress. Gets popularity because of his principles of life.

(X) Has to face displeasure of officers at times. Dislikes flattery. Domestic conditions not very congenial. But comforts of life in a later age. Given to thought of religion and metaphysics.

(XI) Few but reliable friends. Some minor problems of health. May prosper through business. Likely to have very good income.

(XII) Rational attitude of religion. Saves money through a control of expenses. May be troubled by hardships in the initial period of life. But gets good success. May get popularity in some foreign land.

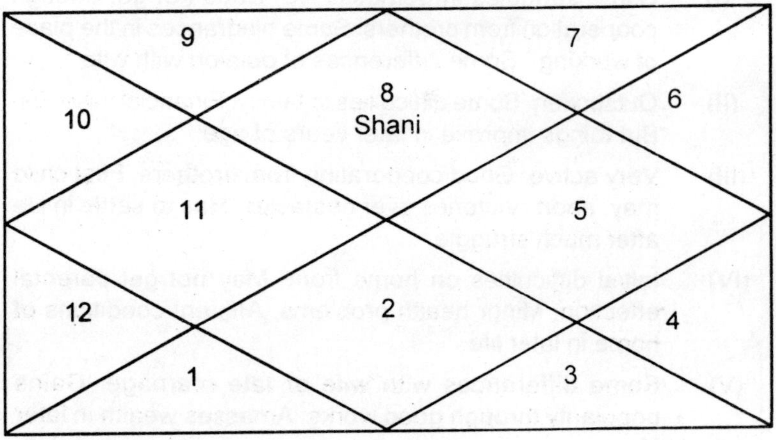

Positions of Rahu in Vrishchik Lagna

House Effects

(I) May need some surgical treatment some time in life. May have a scar on the face. Some differences with wife. Dashing and pushing by nature.

(II) Saves money through fair or foul means. Hard speech. Some disharmonious environment in the family.

(III) Very active and practical. Gets good support from friends belonging to other religion. Capacity of manipulation.

(IV) Gets comforts of domestic life in the sense that one gets the facilities of conveyances and residence. But atmosphere of home may not be to one's heart's content.

(V) Practical intelligence. First progeny may abort. Unexpected opportunities in life. May get a boost from some foreigner.

(VI) Smashes all the obstacles. Has a spirit of fighting back to pay to an opponent in his own coil.

(VII) Very practical wife. May help in furthering mundane career. Wife may belong to some other caste, if caste is given importance.

(VIII) Possibility of an accident. Follows Tamasik religion. Atheistic attitude.

(IX) Mind weaves many plans, some destructive and some constructive. Makes progress by adopting a very practical approach.

(X) Can make progress in the domain of politics. A good capacity of getting one's end served through any means. But may have to wage a war of conflicts in the place of working.

(XI) Earns much after forty-two years of age. May get support from many practical persons. May have good relations with persons of other lands.

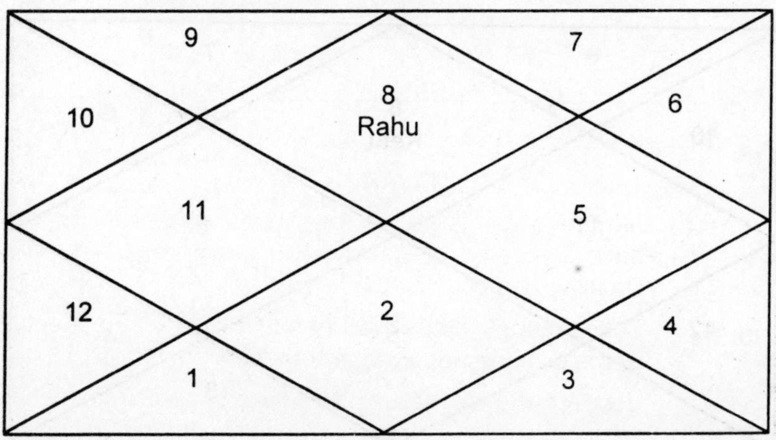

(XII) Can destroy one's enemies in any way. May settle in some foreign land or may profit through their cooperation. Tamasik attitude towards religion.

Positions of Ketu in Vrishchik Lagna

House	Effects
(I)	Good personality. Hot temperament. Brave and outspoken. Capable of destroying intrigues.
(II)	Thoughtful and logical. Good environment in family. Earns money by following good means. Prudent and learned.
(III)	Good relations with brothers. Very active and dashing despite obstacles.
(IV)	Good domestic life. Enjoys all earthly enjoyments. Sober and peaceful atmosphere in home.
(V)	Interest in mystic sciences. Helpful progeny. Children make good progress in life. Gets unexpected chances for betterment in life.
(VI)	Victory over obstacles. May get acknowledgement of some kind of acquirement in some foreign land. Love for occult sciences.
(VII)	Cooperative wife. Progress through partnership. Good personality.
(VIII)	Interested in some occult sciences. Gets money through inheritance.

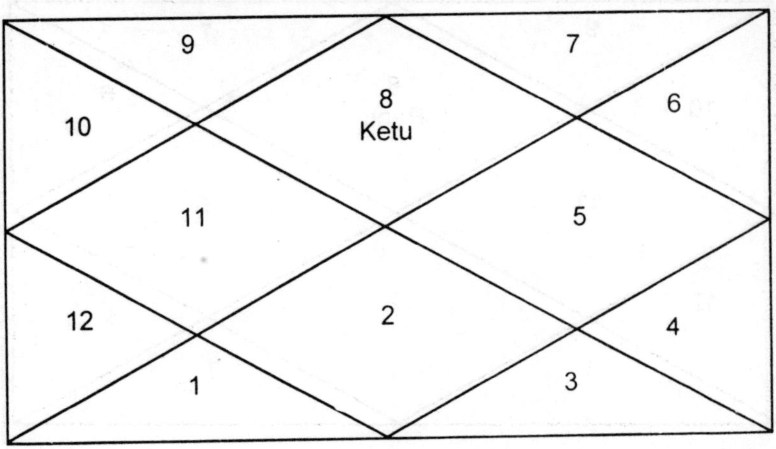

(IX) Mind full of many plannings for life. Gets good success after 46 years of age.

(X) Carves a good career in any field. Peaceful atmosphere in the place of working.

(XI) Very good and cooperative friends. Excellent income after 46 years of age. May shine in business career.

(XII) May get success in some foreign land. Deep interest in occult sciences.

17

DHANU LAGNA

Positions of Surya in Dhanu Lagna

House	Effects
(I)	Very fortunate. May make a good rise in life very early. Difficulties in marriage. Dominating personality. Full of confidence.
(II)	Philosophical interest. Some differences in family. Hard speech. Brings honour to the family. Religious education.
(III)	Very active and fortunate. Gets very good opportunity to settle in life-career between 24 to 28 years of age. Enjoys reputation and influence.
(IV)	Some domestic problem. But comforts of conveyance and residence. Dominates in the field of work.
(V)	Excellent rise in life. Can reach the top position in the domain of politics. A lover of power and prestige.
(VI)	Conflicts in life. But overcomes every impediment to get success. May be self-conceited.
(VII)	Wife non-cooperative. Some problem in adjustment. Good health. Impressive personality.
(VIII)	Philosophical tendency. Loved by father. Spends much due to aristocratic habits. Some problems in family.
(IX)	Very fortunate. Very early start of career. Dominating and confident. General success. Can get good success in politics.
(X)	Exerts influence over fellow workers. Good position. Dominating personality. Some problems in domestic field.

(XI) Has to struggle a lot in building one's career. Cannot get cooperation from officers and persons of influence. But may get benefit from friends from political field.

(XII) May get success in a place away from birthplace. Lives in a royal way. Destroys opposition in a ruthless manner. Worships god or goddess of strength like Hanumana or Durga.

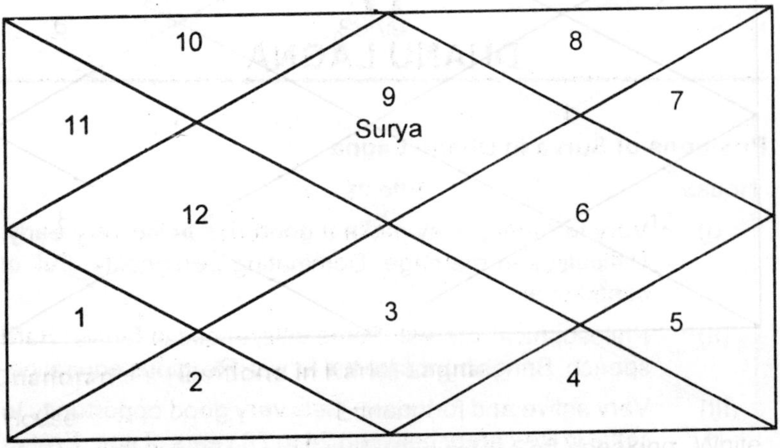

Positions of Chandrama in Dhanu Lagna

House	Effects
(I)	Charming personality. Religious temperament. Beautiful wife. Philosophical attitude towards life.
(II)	Happy family life. Educated. Fluctuating savings. May get inheritance from mother.
(III)	Cool-minded. Secretive. Active. Good relations with sisters. Early settlement of career.
(IV)	Loved by mother. Satisfied household. Facilities of conveyances and good residences. Family lover of religion. Adaptable nature. Practical outlook is not disregarded.
(V)	Obstinate. Persistent. Largeness of egoistic tendency. Female issues more helpful.
(VI)	Fear of conflicts and impediments. Believes in making adjustment. Cheerfulness. Optimistic frame of mind.

(VII) A good capacity of making adjustment. Beautiful personality. Gets good cooperation from all.

(VIII) Very simple hearted. Good longevity. Leaning towards God's devotion. Happy family life. Good education. Tendency to save money.

(IX) A man of principles. Full of self-confidence. Hot temperament. Gets help from fair sex in making a good career. Good relations with brothers and sisters.

(X) Very practical and commercial in outlook. Happy domestic life. Attached to home.

(XI) Very balanced in judging others. Lover of justice and fairplay. May get good earning through pursuit of art.

(XII) Courageous. Hot tempered. Over spends money. Pessimistic outlook. Lover of religious life and literature.

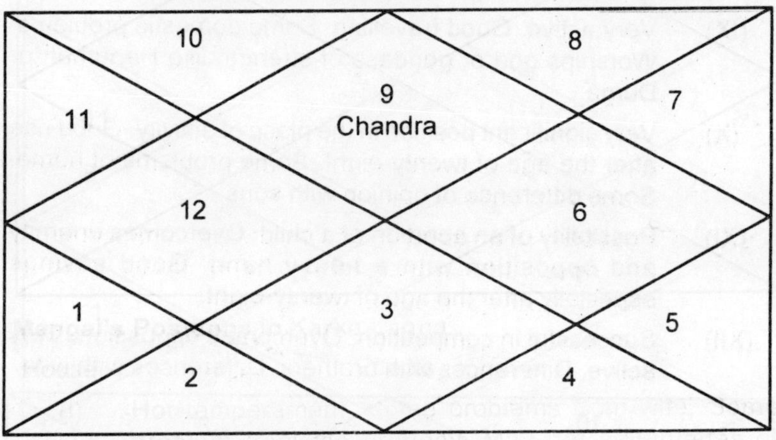

Positions of Mangal in Dhanu Lagna

House Effects

(I) Gets unexpected chances of betterment. Fortunate sons. Gets good popularity. Excessive expenses. Some problems from wife. Landed property.

(II) Very fortunate sons. Very good rise in life. Danger of abortion. Gets unexpected opportunities for betterment.

(III) Very active. Important position in the field of activity. Overcomes opposition and impediments. Gets help from an important person in the rise of life.

(IV) Very important position in the field of activity. Good income comes unexpectedly. Some difference of opinion with wife. Some domestic problems.

(V) Outstanding opportunities of rise in life. Danger of abortion to progeny. Good income after the age of twenty. Danger of an accident. Possibility of intensive travelling.

(VI) Overcomes opposition and impediments. Possibility of surgical treatment. Good rise in life after the age of twenty-eight.

(VII) Delay in marriage. Hot temperament. Good savings despite heavy expenses. Prominent position in the field of action.

(VIII) Possibility of an accident. Good savings through unexpected income. Help from unexpected quarters.

(IX) Very active. Good travelling. Some domestic problems. Worships god or goddess of strength like Hanuman or Durga.

(X) Very significant position in the place of activity. Good rise after the age of twenty-eight. Some problems of home. Some difference of opinion with sons.

(XI) Possibility of an abortion of a child. Overcomes enemity and opposition with a heavy hand. Good savings especially after the age of twenty-eight.

(XII) Successful in competition. Overcomes opposition. Very active. Differences with brothers. Differences with wife.

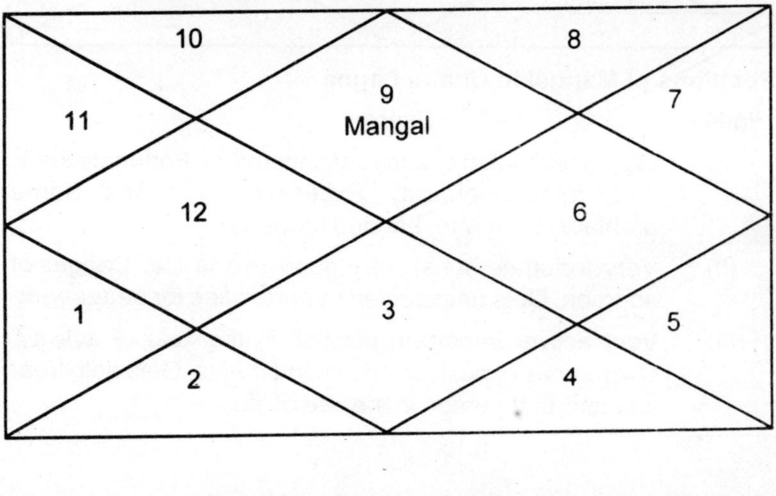

Positions of Shukra in Dhanu Lagna

House	Effects
(I)	Good earning. Charming personality. Beautiful wife. Mixes religion and artistic tendency.
(II)	Very good earning and savings. Good family life. Soft-spoken. Help from some member of fair sex.
(III)	Active. Rational. Thoughtful. A tendency to earn from self-effort. Interested in meditative art and literature.
(IV)	Excellent domestic conditions. Very helpful members of family. Possesses all facilities of residence and conveyances. Cheerful, Sensualistic.
(V)	Helped by members of opposite sex. Girl progeny larger in number. Curt to some extent.
(VI)	Pecuniary impediments in life. But overcomes them through an optimistic attitude of life. Spends money on luxury items.
(VII)	Very charming wife. Beautiful personality. Helped by partners, specially lady partners.
(VIII)	Atheistic attitude. Materialistic philosophy. Enjoys life. Gives importance to comforts of life.
(IX)	Cannot pull on well with opposite sex. Has strict habits of life. Earns through self-effort.
(X)	Happy domestic life. Lacks artistic taste. Commercial view about life.

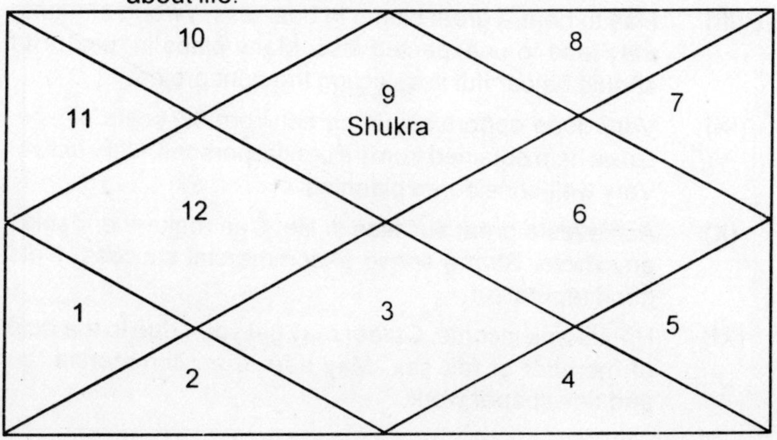

(XI) Very good earning. Can make huge profit through artistic pursuits. Can earn much if cooperation of a member of fair sex is obtained.

(XII) Overspends on luxuries. Tries to enjoy life in a luxurious way. Material pursuits are liked and appreciated.

Positions of Budha in Dhanu Lagna

House	Effects
(I)	Very practical. Very wise. Leaning towards corpolence. Generally speaking good personality. Makes a good worldly progress. Wife too wise and accommodating.
(II)	Earns good amount. Saves pretty well. Good and peaceful family. Good practical education. Good rise after marriage.
(III)	Very active. Activeness brings progress. Good relations with brothers. Good rise after thirty-two years of age.
(IV)	Successful working. May shine in business or journalism. Gets promotions in the field of working.
(V)	Gets unexpected opportunities for progress. Great help from friends. Great help and cooperation from wife or in-laws.
(VI)	Impediments in progress. Ill health of wife. Has to spend on wife and other essential items.
(VII)	Very wise wife. Great success through partnership. Good personality. Very amiable nature.
(VIII)	Has to bear a great slump in business. Wrong planning may lead to unexpected loss. Many plans in mind. But should be careful in selecting the right project
(IX)	Very good opportunity in career from 32 years of age. Great help obtained from influential persons. Very active. Very well-considered planning.
(X)	Achieves a great success in life. Can make friendships anywhere. Strong sense of commercial success. Gets good reputation.
(XI)	Handsome income. Career may get spurt due to the help of member of fair sex. May earn from commercial art and newspaper work.

(XII) Spends money after cool consideration. Business may bring some unexpected loss. Breakdown in business acumen.

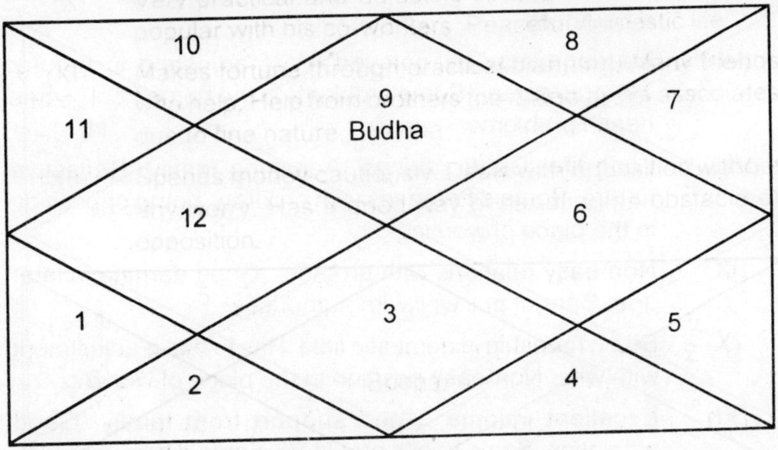

Positions of Shani in Dhanu Lagna

House	Effects
(I)	Philosophical disposition. Wealthy. Tall. Some problems in adjusting with wife. Marriage may be delayed. Very active and self-made. Some initial struggles in the formation of career.
(II)	Wealthy. Happy family life. Interest in reflective religion. Becomes wealthy after the age of 36. Some problems on the domestic front.
(III)	Very active. Popular. Faces struggle with courage and prudence. Difficulties in adjusting with children. Becomes opulent after 35 years of age. Has influential friends.
(IV)	Some problems in domestic region. Lacks mother's affection and protection. Has to face opposition in the working field. Overcomes opposition and impediments with courage. Some problems of health.
(V)	Some problems with married life. Some difference of opinion with children. More enemies than friends. Some hardship in saving.

(VI) Faces opposition and difficulties with patience and wins them. Spends money very carefully. Very active. Good relations with brothers and sisters despite some differences.

(VII) Marriage may be delayed. Wife adjusting in nature. Struggle career. Some problems in the home front. Some health problems.

(VIII) Long life. Good savings. Adjusting family. Reflective nature. Some differences with children. Some opposition in the place of working.

(IX) Non-easy relations with brothers. Good earning in later age. Cannot pull well with authorities.

(X) Some hardship in domestic field. Has to make adjustment with wife. Non-easy position in the place of working.

(XI) Excellent income. Good support from family. Good education. Some health problems. Some differences with progeny.

(XII) Loves peace and meditation. Discards ritualism. Spends savings as one likes.

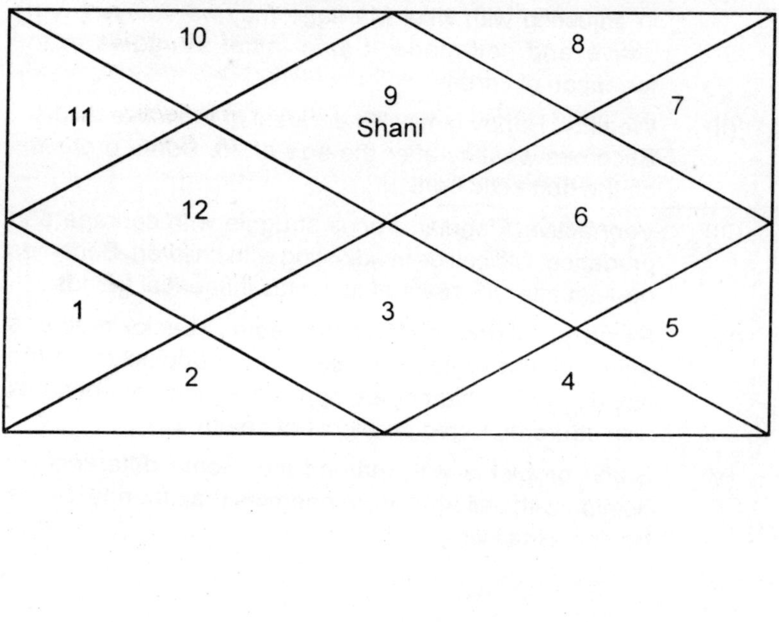

Positions of Guru in Dhanu Lagna

House	Effects
(I)	Very religious minded and learned. Flies in anger on right point. Wife virtuous and beautiful. Tendency to fatness. Lover of sweets.
(II)	Contented family life. Good education. Very religious temperament. Good rise in life. Peaceful environment in the working place. Overcomes obstacles due to devotion to God.
(III)	Career may start from the age of sixteen. Very active. Helpful friends. Devoted life partner.
(IV)	Comfortable domestic atmosphere. Spending on religious items. Fond of pilgrimage. Philosophical temperament.
(V)	Very fortunate and dashing. Permanent source of income. Male issues. Very good health. Early rise in life.
(VI)	Some health problems. Religious tendency. Happy family. Good education. Journeys to religious places.
(VII)	Very good health. Long life. Good source of income. Very popular and active. Good relation with brothers.
(VIII)	Long life. Philosophical bent of mind. Seeker of emancipation. Spends willingly on religious requirements.
(IX)	Very good health. Blessed with sons. Held in respect. Gets unexpected chances of rise in life. Sons bring reputation and position.

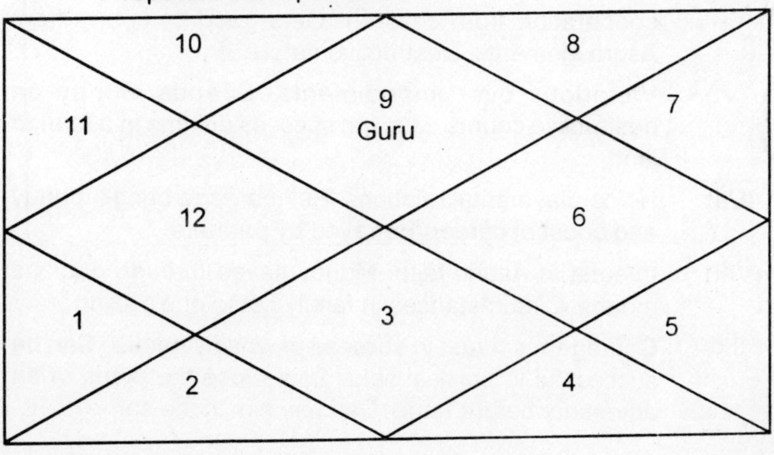

(X) Very happy domestic life. Enjoys mother's affection. Saves money through right means. Good speech and learning.

(XI) Blessed with sons. Dutiful progeny. Good health. Gets friends, cooperation when needed. Efforts generally successful. Good relations with brothers.

(XII) Some health problems. But gets long life. Very religious in outlook. May get success in a place away from the birthplace.

Positions of Rahu in Dhanu Lagna

House Effects

(I) Follows a religion away from the popular religion. Somewhat Tamasik temperament. Good physique. Finds it difficult to make adjustment with wife. May need some surgical treatment.

(II) Good savings. Practical education. Capacity of manoeuvering. Believes in earning through fair or foul means.

(III) Very active. Makes mundane progress. Help received from even Asura elements, i.e., people having rather destructive mentality.

(IV) Gets all the domestic facilities. But there is a sense of disappointment from the domestic atmosphere. Gets progress through struggles.

(V) Rash temperament. First issue may abort. Gets non-cooperation from children. Gets good company from Asura elements. Destructive nature.

(VI) Victorious over impediments. Spends money on destructive counts. May get success or fame in a foreign land.

(VII) No cordial marital relations. But marriage brings money and boost of career. Betrayed by partners.

(VIII) Interest in Asuric faith. Money saved through dubious means. Circumstances in family not to one's liking.

(IX) Courageous thrust in success of worldly nature. Can be successful in political field. Can sense the plans of an adversary before hand. Can pay him in the same coin.

(X) Successful worldly career. Capacity of gaining success through any means. Life full of conflicts.

(XI) Extraordinary earning. Successful man of the world. Diplomatic temperament. Can get success even in the field of politics.

(XII) Overcomes difficulties and obstacles through courage and practical intelligence. Scant regards for religious performances. May shine in a foreign land.

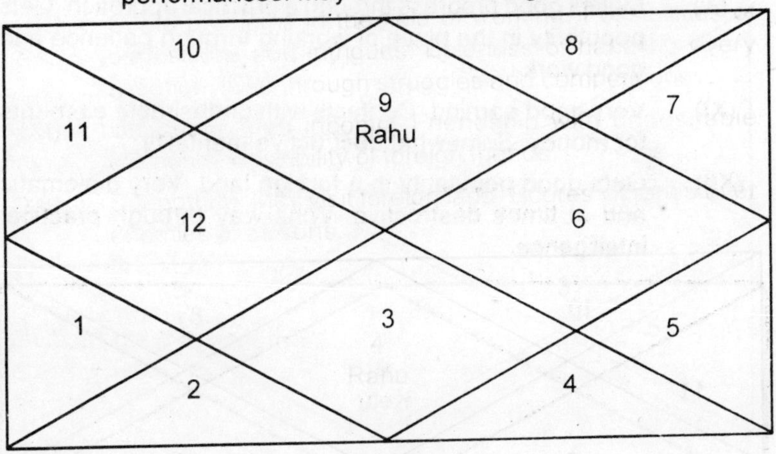

Positions of Ketu in Dhanu Lagna

House	Effects
(I)	Good personality. Love for some occult science. Good natured. Believes in working in a secret way.
(II)	Very good earnings and savings. Good family life. Good education. Good speech.
(III)	Very active and successful. A person who believes in working quietly and sincerely. Good relations with family.
(IV)	Happy domestic life. Members of family live in harmony. Home full of all worldly facilities.
(V)	Deep interest in secret sciences. Sharp intelligence. Aggressive nature. Some differences with children.
(VI)	Conquers all impediments in a very systematic way. May get popularity in foreign land.

(VII) Good married life. Beautiful and obedient wife. May be betrayed by partners if sufficient care is not taken.

(VIII) Deep interest in spirits, ghosts, etc. Believes that they can help in making an advancement in life. Gentle temperament. Good education.

(IX) Very active and can be very successful in the domain of politics due to diplomatic nature. Gets help from unknown quarters.

(X) Makes good progress through a practical approach. Gets popularity in the place of working through patience and good work.

(XI) Very good earning. Contacts with undesirable elements for money. Somewhat destructive mentality.

(XII) Gets good popularity in a foreign land. Very diplomatic and at times destructive. Wins way through practical intelligence.

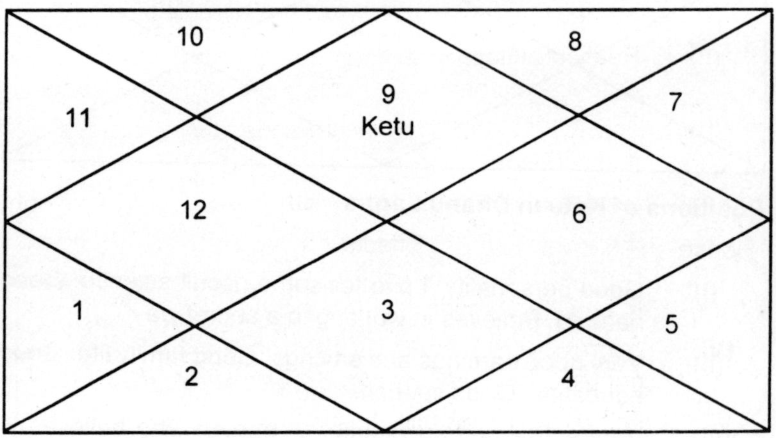

18

MAKARA LAGNA

Positions of Surya in Makara Lagna

House	Effects
(I)	Majestic personality. Hurdles in marriage. If married, adjustment with wife not easy. Hot temperament. Somewhat tense relations with sons.
(II)	Rational attitude. Habit of pondering over truth. Educated. Smooth environment in family. May get father's property.
(III)	Active. Fortunate. Influential friends. Respect for teachers and scriptures.
(IV)	Enjoys luxuries supplied by father. Interest in philosophy and religion. Fond of following set principles.
(V)	First child may abort. Religious interest. Fame. Obstinate to an extent. Disdains flattery.
(VI)	Scores over enemies. Pushes back impediments. May get fame in a foreign land. Spends in a royal way.
(VII)	Impressive personality. Hot nature. Adjustment with wife rather difficult. May get father's favour.
(VIII)	Deep religious temperament. Gets parental inheritance. Educated. Good environment in family.
(IX)	Very active. Good relation with brothers. Gets cooperation from some political leaders in the betterment of career.
(X)	Gets prominent position in the field of working. Some problems in domestic set-up. Some uneasy relations with father.

(XI) Good income. Help from political friends. Assertive nature. Strong minded person.

(XII) Spends money lavishly. Deep interest in religion. Can make advance in the field of meditation.

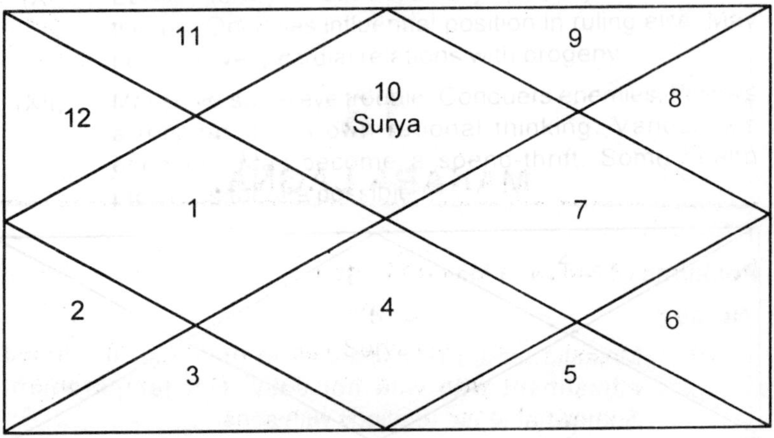

Positions of Chandrama in Makara Lagna

House	Effects
(I)	Tall. A sense of despondence prevails in mind. Mind rather full of changing thoughts. Loves wife. Wife beautiful.
(II)	Man of action. Marriage brings luck. Good education. Good speech. Never unveils one's plans.
(III)	Very religious temperament. Dutiful and obedient wife. Good relations with brothers. Practical outlook.
(IV)	Obstinate. Man of iron will. Happy domestic conditions. Smooth sailing in the field of working.
(V)	Haughty. Very pretty wife. Female issues more in number. Wife lucky for life.
(VI)	Adjusting nature. Wife suffers from occasional ailments. Indecisive mind. Love for writing or journalism.
(VII)	Very pretty wife. Wife quite adjusting in nature. A person of fine sentiments. Mind easily assailed by sorrow and gladness.
(VIII)	Love for religion. Good education. Fine speech. Iron will. Has fixed views. Full of self-confidence.

(IX) Practical mind. Adjusting nature. Wife brings money. Very religious outlook, although religious views are orthodox.

(X) Very balanced mind. Lover of justice. Lovers of fine arts and literature. Witty. Very popular and even-minded. Good domestic environment.

(XI) Easily flies in anger. Biting speech. Wife brings money. Adjustment with others rather difficult. But help comes from friends when needed.

(XII) Spends lavishly on religious issues. Performs many religious rites. Makes frequent journeys to religious places. A lover of justice and morality.

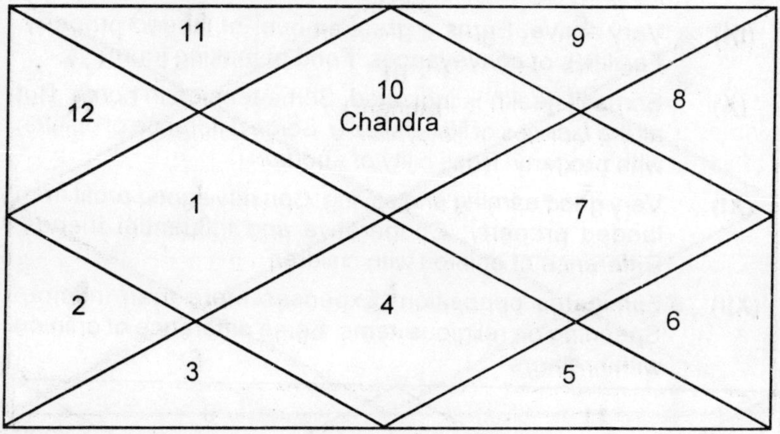

Positions of Mangala in Makara Lagna

House Effects

(I) Warrior-like temperament. Courageous. Aggressive. Dominating. Excellent income. All domestic facilities. Affection of the mother. But difference of opinion with wife.

(II) First child may abort. Good savings. Betterment after the age of 28. Inheritance from father.

(III) Very active. Religious minded. Gets importance in the place of working. Some conflicts in the working place possible. May get unexpected opportunities in life for betterment.

(IV) All domestic facilities. Ample landed property. Excellent help from friends. Married life may not be very happy.

(V) Help and cooperation from friends. Good income through their help. May gain much through land. Possibility of some accident.

(VI) Victorious over impediments and opposition. Spends much. May be fond of travelling.

(VII) Possibility of some surgical operations. Married life may not be very satisfactory. Gains importance in the place of working. Some tensions in the family circle.

(VIII) Some differences in the family environment. Good income. Some differences with brothers.

(IX) Very active. Earns a great amount of landed property. Facilities of conveyances. Fond of making journeys.

(X) Some ill health is indicated. Some tension in home. But all the facilities of life available. Some difference of opinion with progeny. Possibility of abortion.

(XI) Very good earning and saving. Can have good profit from landed property. Cooperative and influential friends. Difference of opinion with children.

(XII) Eliminates opposition. Expenses more than income. Spending on religious items. Some difference of opinion with brothers.

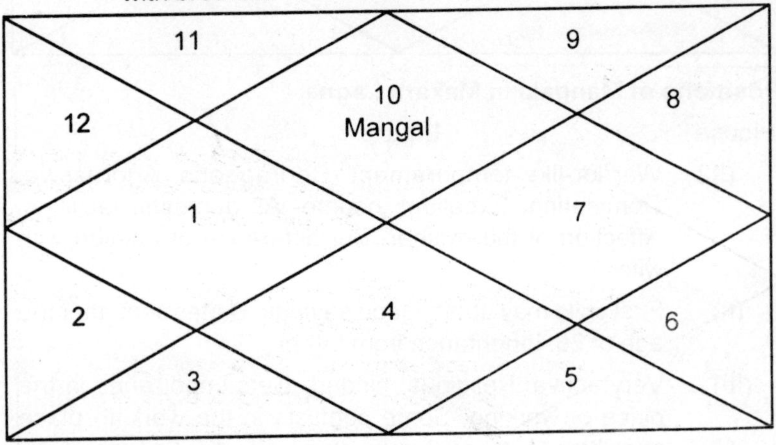

Positions of Shukra in Makara Lagna

House	Effects
(I)	Very charming personality of wife. Good physical build. Lovable nature. Good progeny. Amiable nature.
(II)	Good savings. Good education. Happy family environment. Cooperative relatives. Sweet speech.
(III)	Good progress in profession. Good chances of advancement. Settles in life rather early. Loved by ladies. Fond of artistic pursuits.
(IV)	Happy domestic life. Smooth sailing in the place of working. Enjoys popularity.
(V)	Sweet tongued. Amiable children. Can shine in any artistic or literary vocation. Good earnings.
(VI)	Conflict-free life. Spends on luxuries. Comfortable living. May have to face some impediments in furthering one's career.
(VII)	Very charming personality. Very beautiful wife. Married life quite happy. Loved by ladies.
(VIII)	Educated. Fond of worldly pleasures. Good savings. Happy family. May shine in one's profession after some struggles.
(IX)	Very practical. Good relations with brothers. Settles in life quite early: May get fame.

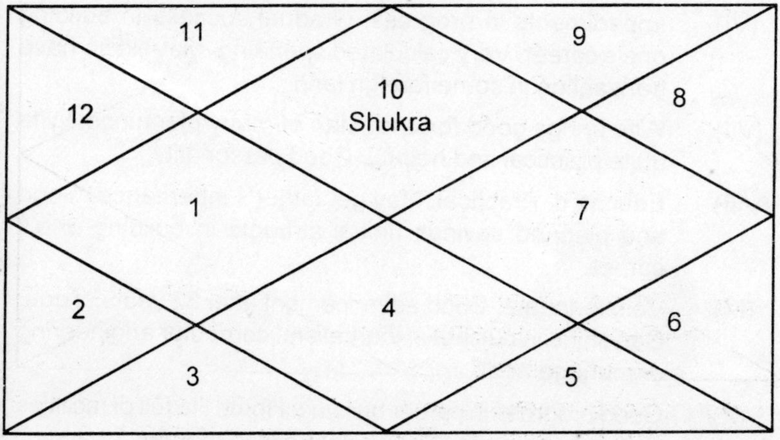

(X) Very good progress in career. Smooth sailing in career. Happy domestic environment. All domestic comforts.

(XI) Good income. But some conflicts in earning. Loved by progeny. But some difference of opinion possible. Cooperation from friends.

(XII) Prosperous and comfortable life. Spends lavishly to enjoy life. Hedonistic philosophy. Fond of making pleasure journeys.

Positions of Budha in Makara Lagna

House	Effects
(I)	Good personality. Practical. Adjusting. Fortunate. Good looking and wise Wife. May prosper through partnership.
(II)	Educated. Man of action and not mere words. Family life peaceful. Good savings. May face some impediment in saving due to enemies. Sweet tongued.
(III)	Very active. Builds career through self-effort. May prosper in journalism or management. Good career after 32 years of age.
(IV)	Happy domestic life. Smooth sailing in the place of working. Domestic facilities available.
(V)	Unexpected chance of betterment. Good relations with children. Practical intelligence. Does not like empty idealism.
(VI)	Impediments in progress. Gradual success in building one's career. Very calculated spending. May like to have transaction in some foreign land.
(VII)	Wife brings good fortune. Man of many plannings. Wife quite practical and helpful. Good personality.
(VIII)	Educated. Practical. May get father's inheritance. Good and planned savings. Initial struggle in building one's career.
(IX)	Very fortunate. Good advancement after 32 years of age. Can shine in business, journalism, computer engineering or management.
(X)	Good progress in career building. Home life full of facilities and conveyances. Good relation with mother.

(XI) Can shine in business of some kind through friends' help or cooperation. Good relation with progeny. Practical approach in dealing with others.

(XII) Makes progress through impediments. May enter into some business deal with any foreign firm. Spends money in a well-calculated way.

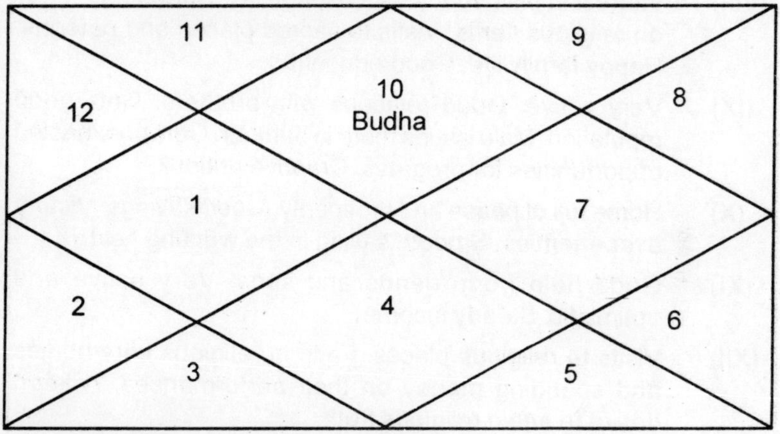

Positions of Guru in Makara Lagna

House Effects

(I) Good personality. Religious-minded wife and children. Gradual rise in life and prestige. Rational attitude in religion. May be required to spend money in excess to income.

(II) Very rational approach in the domain of religion. Interest in philosophy and occult sciences. Good family environment. Helpful relatives.

(III) Very active and God-fearing. Attains good position through devotion to God. Very helpful brothers and friends.

(IV) Very much faith in religious matters. Indulges in making journeys and religious performances. Happy home. Smooth sailing in profession.

(V) Helpful friends. Gradual rise in income. Good health, but a tendency towards corpolence. Fond of sweet dishes.

(VI) Scrupulous in spending money. Spending money on religious ceremonies. Visits to sacred places. Steadiness in profession.

(VII) Excellent relations with brothers. Very active and successful. Steady income. Good health.

(VIII) Interest in philosophy. Good longevity. Spending money on religious items. Visits to sacred places and persons. Happy family life. Good education.

(IX) Very active. Good relations with brothers. Gets good reputation. Male issues more in number. Gets unexpected opportunities for progress. Creative outlook.

(X) Home full of peace and prosperity. Good savings. Victory over enemies. Smooth sailing in the working field.

(XI) Good help from friends and sons. Very active and optimistic. Steady income.

(XII) Visits to religious places. Faith in religious ceremonies and spending money on their performances. A keen desire to attain religious truth.

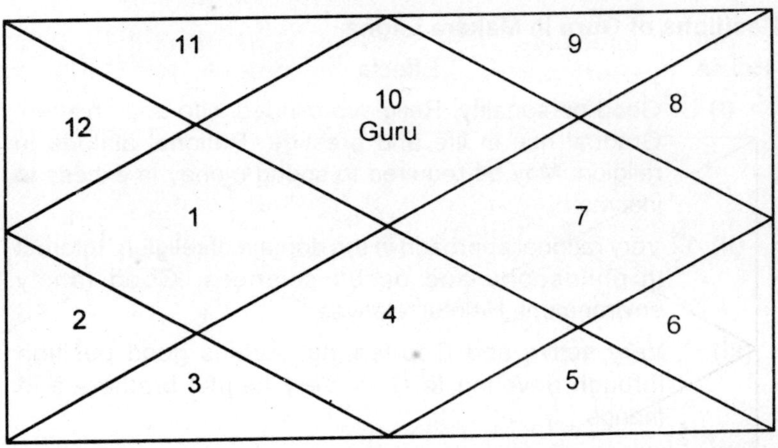

Positions of Shani in Makara Lagna

House	Effects
(I)	Good longevity. Good health. Makes progress in one's profession in a delayed way. Later part of life more enjoyable than the first one. Some difference of opinion with life-partner. There may be delay in marriage.
(II)	Good savings in later life. Love for occult science. Happy family life. Good education.
(III)	Good advance in life after the age of 36. Good relations with brothers. Some difference of opinion with children. Some conflicts in money earning in the initial life.
(IV)	Dissatisfaction from home. Domestic life full of problems. May be required to leave one's home. Lacks mother's affection. Some problems concerning health. Score victories over problems and impediments.
(V)	Delay in marriage. Problems concerning children. Insufficient earnings. Difficulties in savings.
(VI)	Some problems concerning life and health. Interest in philosophical thinking. Uneasy relations with brothers.
(VII)	Impediments in progress. Good health. Problems concerning family. Marriage may be delayed. Differences with wife.

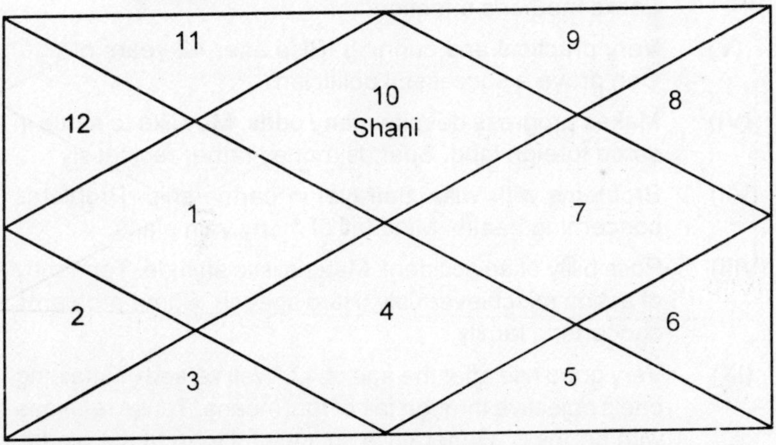

(VIII) Long life, although there may be ill health in childhood. Saves money with difficulty. Tensions in the working place. Differences with children.

(IX) Very good health. Very good savings in life. All domestic facilities. Relations with wife on the whole good, but occasional differences, cannot be ruled out. May establish good relations with the residents of foreign lands.

(X) Unhelpful friends. Difficulties in good earnings. Bad relations with children. Some problems concerning health.

(XI) Deep philosophical interest. May settle in some foreign land. Good relations with persons belonging to foreign nations. Handles impediments with fortitude.

Positions of Rahu in Makara Lagna

House	Effects
(I)	Good personality. Some health problem. Differences with wife. Craftiness. Diplomatic. Rise after 42 years of age.
(II)	Good savings. Practical thinking. Some dissensions in family. Faith in Tamasik religion.
(III)	Very active. Strained relations with brothers. Does not care for morality. Believes in attaining one's objective through any means.
(IV)	Dissatisfied home. Some problems in the profession. Lacks mother's affection.
(V)	Very practical and cunning. Rise after 42 years of age. Can prove a successful politician.
(VI)	Makes progress despite many odds. May like to settle in some foreign land. Spends money rather recklessly.
(VII)	Problems with wife. Betrayal in partnership. Problems concerning health. Mind full of many vain plans.
(VIII)	Possibility of an accident. Materialistic attitude. Tendency of action mischieveously. Hard speech. Some problems concerning family.
(IX)	Very good rise after the age of 42. Well versed in attaining one's objective through fair or foul means. Tense relations with brothers. Generally a successful man of the world.

(X) Some domestic problems. Uneasy relations with fellow workers. Selfish tendency. But worldly success.

(XI) Non-cordial relations with friends. Selfish mentality. Betrayal by friends possible. Income comes through Tamasik means.

(XII) Victory over calamities and impediments. May settle in some foreign land. May gain through dealings with foreign firms or persons.

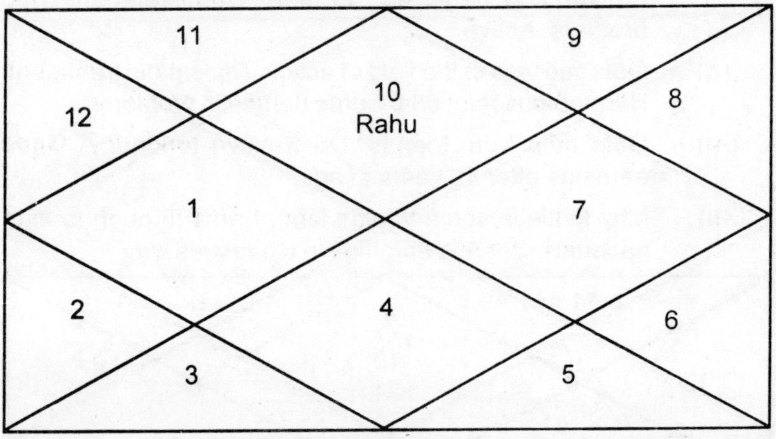

Positions of Ketu in Makara Lagna

House Effects

(I) Good personality. Man of words. Intelligent. Learned. Lover of an occult science.

(II) Happy family. Members of family cooperative. Saves enormous amount of money. Lover of philosophy.

(III) Lover of some occult science. Active . Religious nature. Good relations with brothers. Earns good money after 46 years of age.

(IV) Some problems of family. Lacks mother's affection. Enjoys all the comforts of home.

(V) Diplomatic. Helped by friends. Congenial. Good relations with children.

(VI) Surmounts impediments in a diplomatic manner. Good relations with some national of a foreign land. Spends money cautiously.

(VII) Good and helping wife. May earn through partnership. Good physique but there may be some health problem.

(VIII) Runs after Tamasik religion. Interest in occult subjects.

(IX) Earns profusely after 46 years of age. May get unexpected helpers in fortune. Good relations with brothers. Active.

(X) Gets success in the field of action. Diplomatic treatment. Harmonious relations. Some domestic problems.

(XI) Gets help from friends. Destructive tendency. Good earnings after 46 years of age.

(XII) May settle in some foreign land. Earns through foreign nationals. Spends earnings in a cautious way.

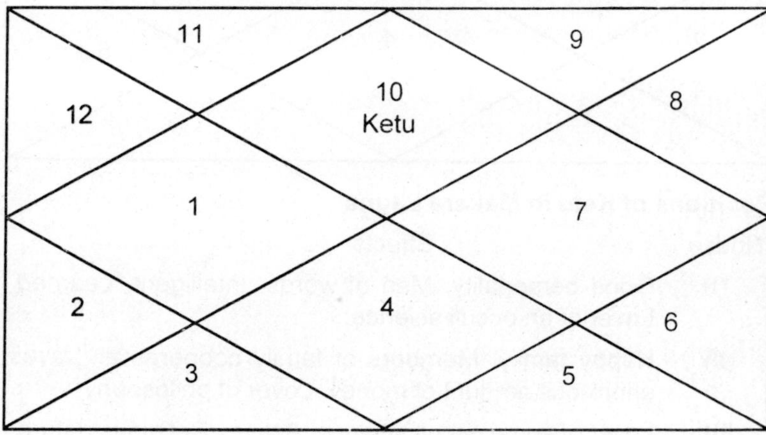

19

KUMBHA LAGNA

Positions of Surya in Kumbha Lagna

House	Effects
(I)	Commanding personality. Delay in marriage. Wife dominating. Interest in philosophy and rational religion.
(II)	Educated. Deeply religious. Man of principles. Gets inheritance from father. Good atmosphere in family.
(III)	Very active and successful. Relations with influential leaders and persons. Wife comes from a commanding community. She is very helpful in husband's success.
(IV)	Some problems in domestic circle. Commands influence in the place of activity. Enjoys domestic facilities.
(V)	Good and helpful friends. Good relations with children. But there is a possibility of abortion. Practical intelligence.
(VI)	Ruins enemies. Not deterred by calamities. Commands influence in the field of activity.
(VII)	Very successful in the domain of politics. Wife has dominating temperament and comes from a higher strata of society. Some problems concerning health.
(VIII)	Deeply religious. Gets paternal property. Educated. Good influence in the family.
(IX)	Wife non-adjusting. Problems from political or higher circles. But settles in life in the early twenties.
(X)	Good support from wife and friend who are political leaders. Wields influence in the domain of one's activity. Gets all domestic facilities.

(XI) Marriage brings good luck. Wife helpful in the earnings or her relatives may be helpful in earnings. Religious minded wife.

(XII) Lives in a royal manner. Does not care for expenses. May cultivate good relations with some foreign nationals. Makes progress despite obstacles.

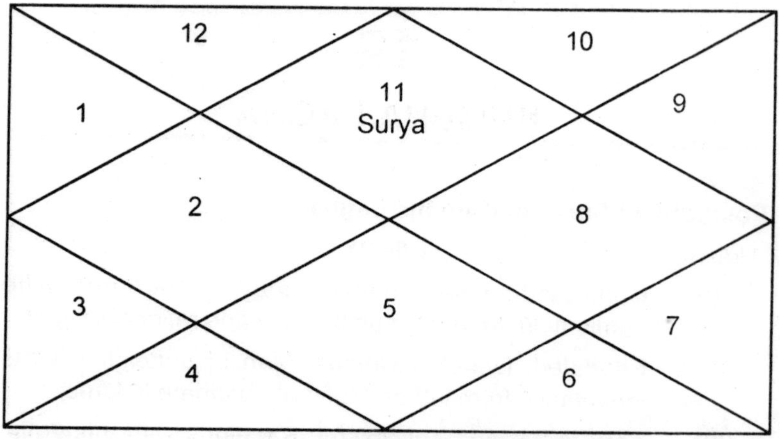

Positions of Chandrama in Kumbha Lagna

House	Effects
(I)	Charming personality. Thoughtful temperament. Wife, too, good looking. Not easily perturbed.
(II)	Very religious minded. Simple habits. Good atmosphere in family. Educated. Pretty face.
(III)	Obstinate. Man of iron will. Very active. Reaches top position in any walk of life through self-effort.
(IV)	Good domestic environment. Occasional difficulties. But cheerful temperament.
(V)	Can adjust with every person. Learned. Loves progeny. Helpful friends. Female children more in number.
(VI)	Occasional troubles from enemies. But all difficulties vanish in course of time. Easily excitable. Very sensitive.
(VII)	A man of courage: Follows one's principles rigidly. Loves wife. Good personality.

(VIII) Love for religion. Practical. Good family environment. Loved by family.

(IX) A man of balanced attitude. Lover of justice. Good relations with brothers and sisters.

(X) Cannot adjust with everybody. May fly in anger easily. Cannot forget acts of enemies. Good family environment. Cannot have very smooth relations with fellow persons.

(XI) Friends not very helpful. They may bring problems. Religious persons give help. Earning through moral means.

(XII) Fond of travelling. Overspends money. May pick up good relations with some foreign national.

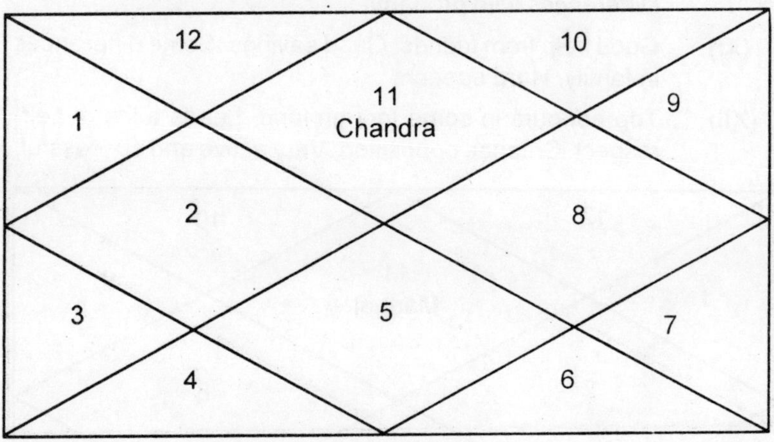

Positions of Mangal in Kumbha Lagna

House Effects

(I) Good personality. A man of few words. Studious temperament. Wife beautiful. Ailing tendency.

(II) Deeply religious. Educated. Good family environment. Finds difficulty in saving money.

(III) A man of strong will. A deep sense of self-respect. Very active and energetic. Makes progress through self-effort.

(IV) Some domestic problems. Gets enough importance in the place of activity. Some difference of opinion with wife.

(V) Gets unexpected help from friends. Has good relations with persons of foreign origin. Possibility of abortion.

(VI) Overcome opposition. Spends lavishly. Forces way to success through struggle.

(VII) Hot temper. Prominent position in the place of working. Good savings. Some differences in the family.

(VIII) Very active. Self-respect is the top value. Devotion to Devi or Hanuman or any other deity of strength.

(IX) Some differences with brothers. Some differences in the domestic field.

(X) Holds a very good administrative or important position. Enjoys respect and honour. Enemies cannot prevail. Differences with progeny.

(XI) Good help from friends. Good savings. Some differences in family. Hard speech.

(XII) Top honours in some foreign land. Leads a life of self-respect. Crushes opposition. Very active and successful.

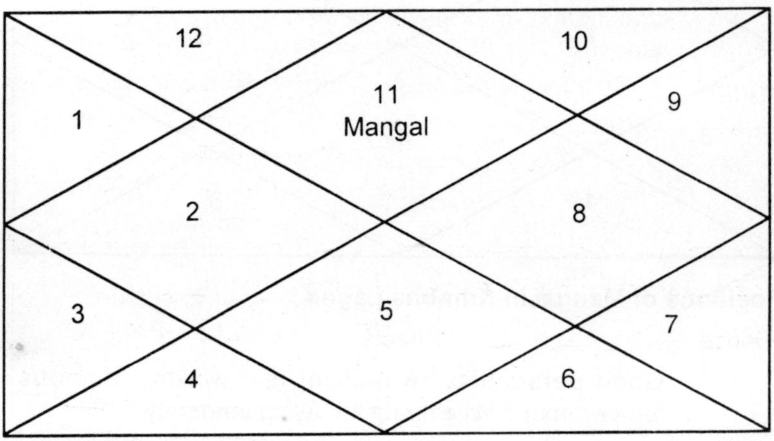

Positions of Shukra in Kumbha Lagna

House	Effects
(I)	Beautiful personality. Very fortunate. Rise in the early twenties of life. Pretty wife. Educated.
(II)	Very fortunate. Success comes with little effort. Good savings and earnings. Materialistic philosophy of life.
(III)	Fortunate. Successful efforts. Good relations with brothers and sisters.
(IV)	Very good domestic conditions. All the domestic facilities of residence and conveyances. Happy conditions in the place of working.
(V)	Practical intelligence. Successful worldly life. Good relations with progeny. Girls progeny more in number.
(VI)	Overcomes impediments. Initial struggles for establishing career. Spends lavishly on luxuries. Constantly thinking about the opposite sex.
(VII)	Charming personality. Happy married life. Wife dominating. May get help from some political female leader.
(VIII)	Scant respect for religion. Struggles in building proper career. Education with difficulty.
(IX)	Very fortunate. Gets help of some lady friend in pushing one's career. Happy conditions in home. Good relations with relatives.

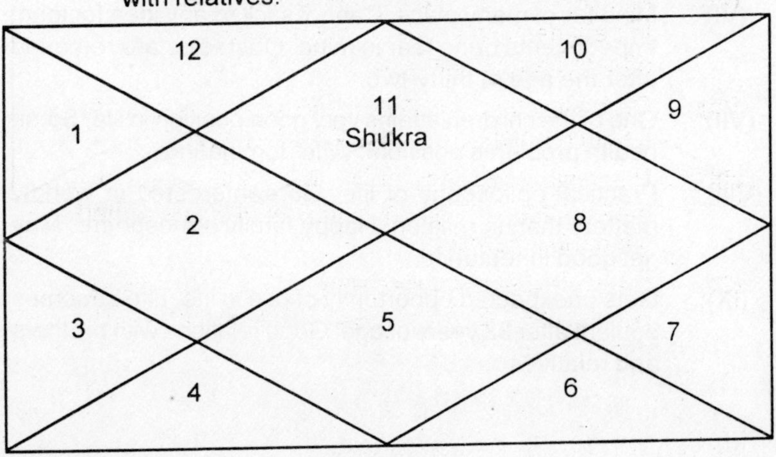

(X) Good conditions in the place of working. On the whole tolerably good home conditions. Facilities of conveyance and good residence.

(XI) Steady income. Good help from progeny. Girl friends helpful. Income from items of luxuries.

(XII) Spends heavily on luxuries. Fond of travelling for pleasure. May develop good relations with persons of foreign origin.

Positions of Budha in Kumbha Lagna

House	Effects
(I)	Good personality. Lover of profound thinking. Does not like to divulge every idea. Secretive. Wife practical and helpful.
(II)	Children may not be obedient. Still family atmosphere is good. Love for religion. Gets some unexpected chance of good earning in life.
(III)	Active. Lucky. Birth of a child may bring luck. A good planner. Early rise in life.
(IV)	Good domestic conditions. Facilities of good residence and conveyance. Cooperative relatives. Conditions in the place of working satisfactory.
(V)	Very intelligent. Children bring good luck. Gets many unexpected chances of progress.
(VI)	Mind full of many plans. Cannot stick to any idea for long. Impediments bring fear in mind. Obstacles are removed after the age of thirty-two.
(VII)	One of the children attains very good position in life. Some health problems possible. Wife dominating.
(VIII)	Practical philosophy of life. More interested in worldly matters than in religion. Happy family atmosphere. May get good inheritance.
(IX)	Gets unexpected opportunity of rise in life. Life becomes opulent after 32 years of age. Good relations with brothers and relatives.

(X) Some obstacles in progress. Some problems in dealing with fellow workers or friends. Dissolves problems through a well-planned methodology.

(XI) Children bring rise in income. Unexpected chances of rise in life. Helpful friends. A tendency to do business.

(XII) Very economical. Spends money carefully. Travelling in commercial cities. Strained relations with children.

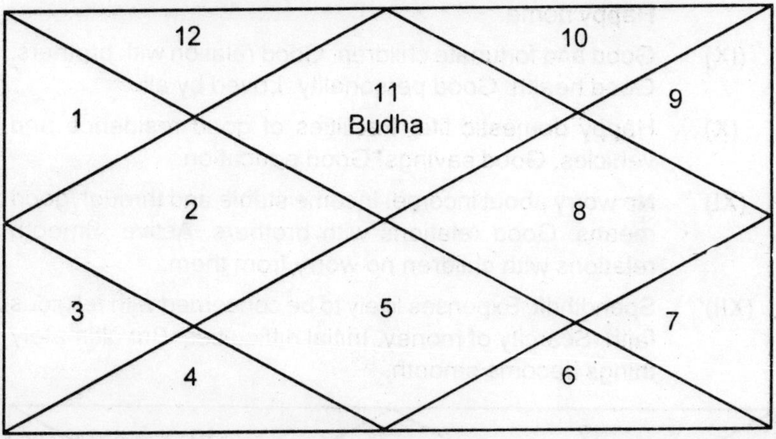

Positions of Guru in Kumbha Lagna

House	Effects
(I)	Wealthy. Good personality. Obedient and religious-minded wife. First born child is likely to be a son. Children obedient and brilliant. Early settlement of career. Thoughtful.
(II)	Good savings. Happy family. Cooperative relatives. Good education. Interest in religion and morality.
(III)	Very good earning through right means. Stability in earning. Helpful and pious-minded friends. Sober wife.
(IV)	Some problems concerning home. Smoothness in the place of working. Expenses on religious items and performances. Pilgrimages.
(V)	Good stable earning. Very helpful friends. Good health. Success in efforts of building career.

(VI) Danger of incurring debts. Difficulties in good earning. Fondness for visits to religious places. Ultimate deliverence from debts and impediments.

(VII) Good health. Good relation with brothers and friends. Help comes from friends. Good wife.

(VIII) Very good savings through right means. Deep interest in religion and philosophy. Good longevity. Popularity. Happy home.

(IX) Good and fortunate children. Good relation with brothers. Good health. Good personality. Loved by all.

(X) Happy domestic life. Facilities of good residence and vehicles. Good savings. Good education.

(XI) No worry about income. Income stable and through good means. Good relations with brothers. Active. Smooth relations with children no worry from them.

(XII) Spendthrift. Expenses likely to be concerned with religious faith. Scarcity of money. Initial difficulties. But ultimately things become smooth.

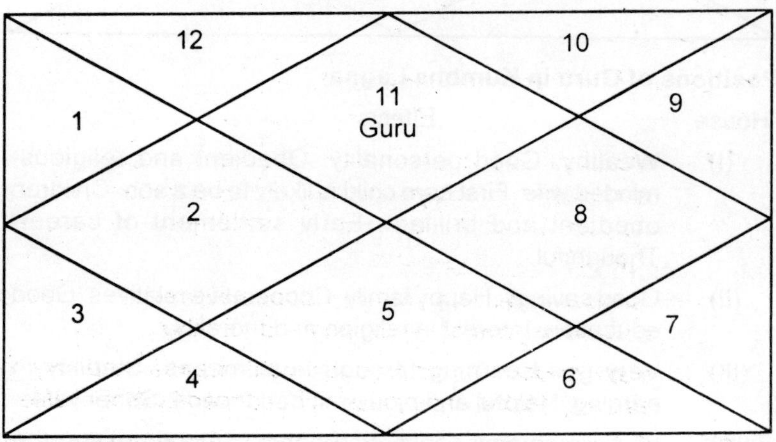

Positions of Shani in Kumbha Lagna

House	Effects
(I)	Long life. Health may not be satisfactory in the initial period of life. Thoughtful. Delay in marriage or dissatisfaction from wife. Not very cordial relations with brothers. Some differences in the working place.
(II)	Religious education. Some problems in home. Good income, but savings not possible to a desirable extent.
(III)	Strained relations with brothers. Unsteady relations with progeny. Danger of abortion. Good rise after the age of thirty-six.
(IV)	Some problems in home. Some problems in the place of working. Cannot be defeated by enemies despite their efforts to do so. Good longevity.
(V)	Children brilliant. Differences with wife. Differences with friends. Savings possible only after the age of thirty-six.
(VI)	Overcomes impediments and obstacles. Faith in rational religion. Fond of journey. May be required to settle away from home or birthplace.
(VII)	Delay in marriage. Of strong differences with wife. Health is likely to be dissatisfactory. Impediments in progress. Problems in home.
(VIII)	Long life. Fond of rational thinking and philosophy. Differences with members of family. Differences with officers and fellow workers in the place of working.
(IX)	Very good health. Good circle of friends. Capacity of thinking independently and acting accordingly.
(X)	Cannot have smooth relations in the place of working. Domestic conditions not satisfactory. Bad relations with wife. Heavy expenses.
(XI)	Very helpful friends. Good health. Children brilliant although not very helpful. Deep faith in philosophical thinking.

(XII) Heavy expenses. May get renown in some foreign land. Overcomes obstacles and impediments.

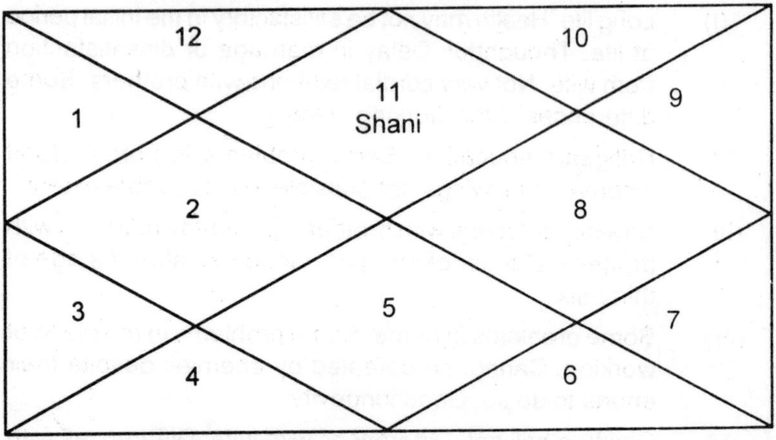

Positions of Rahu in Kumbha Lagna

House	Effects
(I)	Good personality. Talkative. Face may have a scar. Cunning. Does not divulge his plan. May succeed in diplomatic missions.
(II)	Unorthodox. Impediments in education. Members of family do not cooperate.
(III)	Very active. Does not have smooth relations with brothers. Very practical and at times aggressive.
(IV)	Domestic field full of impediments. Domestic conditions improve a lot after the age of forty-two.
(V)	First born child may abort. Very intelligent from the standpoint of worldly affairs. Rises to a great height through some unexpected chance in life. May have good dealings with foreigners.
(VI)	Mind full of destructive plans. Overcomes enemies through cunning moves. Shines where political tendency counts.
(VII)	Wife non-cooperative. Marriage is likely to be untraditional. Partners not reliable.

(VIII) Faith in Tamasik religion. Obstacles in education. Some problems in family. Unexpected inheritance.

(IX) Very diplomatic. Can shine in the field of political plannings. Can adopt destructive ways to win one's objective.

(X) Conflicts and differences in the field of working. Believes in achieving one's objectives through cunning moves.

(XI) Friendship with antisocial elements. Friends apparently religious minded but actually have destructive tendencies.

(XII) May settle in a place distant from the birthplace. Expenses on destructive plannings. Does not care for religious and moral values.

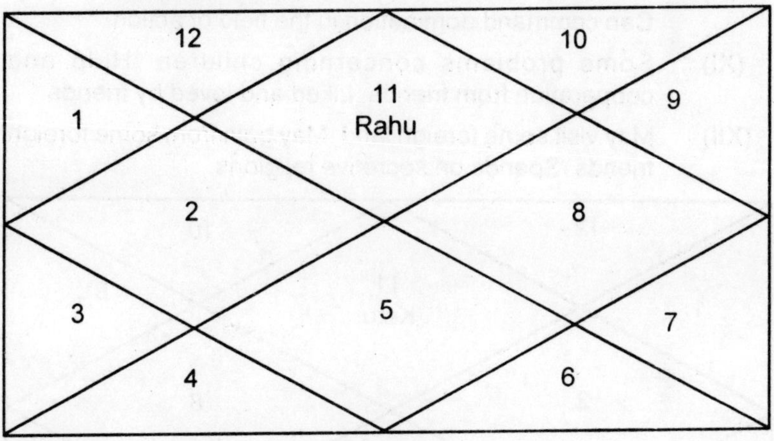

Positions of Ketu in Kumbha Lagna

House	Effects
(I)	Good personality. Sober and thoughtful. Modest. Secretive. Problems from wife.
(II)	Good savings. Good education. Interest in secret lores. Good family environment.
(III)	Active. Successful in achieving one's objective. Good relations with brothers. Gets success by taking initiatives in one's field.
(IV)	Domestic life happy. All the domestic facilities like good residence and conveyances.

(V) Intelligent. Educated. Good progeny. Unexpected chances of betterment. Friends may not be reliable.

(VI) Overcomes obstacles and impediments through practical intelligence. Spends money through due consideration.

(VII) Defeats enemies. Overcomes impediments. Tactful. Concentrates on action than on thought. Wife dominating. Hidden danger from partners.

(VIII) Interest in secretive religion. Family atmosphere not very cooperative. Savings made in a secret manner.

(IX) Good relations with brothers. Tactful. Liked by ladies. Popular. Makes good rise after the age of 46.

(X) Problems of home. Acts tactfully in the field of activity. Can command domination in the field of action.

(XI) Some problems concerning children. Help and cooperation from friends. Liked and loved by friends.

(XII) May visit some foreign land. May gain from some foreign friends. Spends on secretive religions.

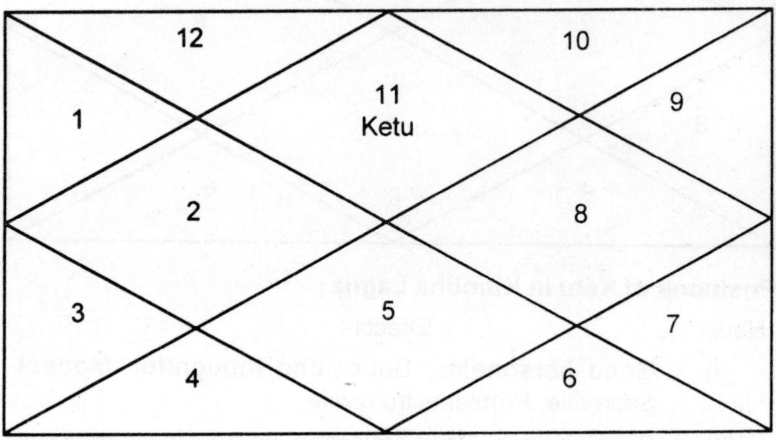

20

MEENA LAGNA

Positions of Surya in Meena Lagna

House	Effects
(I)	Problems of ill health. Hot temperament. Adjustment with wife becomes a tough problem. Delay in marriage likely.
(II)	Conquerer of enemies. Can shine in the political field. Educated. Savings with difficulty. Gains from enemies.
(III)	Very active. Gets success in attempts for making strides in life. Good and influential brothers.
(IV)	Some domestic problems possible. Commanding position in the field of activity. May not enjoy mother's affection.
(V)	Differences with children. Danger of abortion of a child. Intelligent. Educated. Friends may be found wanting in cooperation and help.
(VI)	Subdues every opposition in a strong manner. Good relations with authoritative people. Spends money in a royal way.
(VII)	Delay in marriage. Differences with wife. Good personality. Partners may not be found reliable.
(VIII)	Interest in rational religion. Spiritual attitude. May get inheritance. Relations with father may not be cordial.
(IX)	Makes great progress through self-effort and cooperation of people of authority. Good relations with brothers. Good rise from the age of twenty-eight.
(X)	Occupies position of authority and influence. Proves a good and competent administrative officer. Holds a position of authority in the field of activity.

(XI) Earns money through great effort. Gets help from some leader or a person holding good position. May not be very popular.

(XII) Gets good popularity. Defeats opposition. Spends money in a very thoughtful manner. May establish good relation with influential persons of a foreign land.

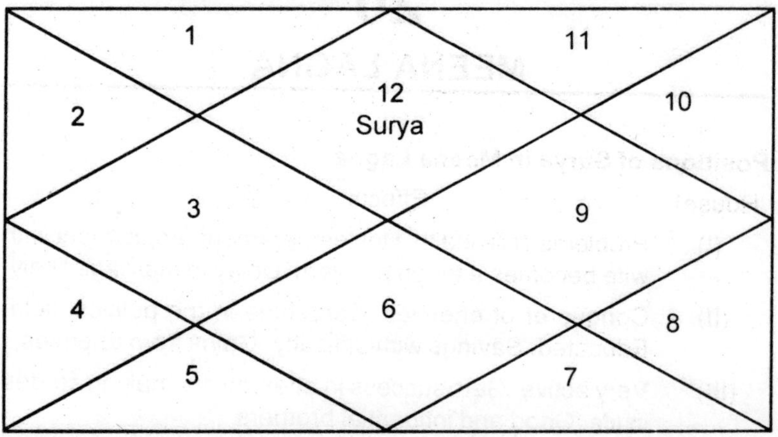

Positions of Chandrama in Meena Lagna

House Effects

(I) Charming personality. Beautiful wife. Amiable nature. Liked by people. Adjusting nature.

(II) Gets some unexpected opportunity of making progress in life. Progeny brings money and prestige. Obstinate nature. Danger of abortion of a child.

(III) Very cheerful temperament. Gets an unexpected opportunity that gives fame and progress. Does not care for opposition.

(IV) Adjusting nature. Peaceful domestic environment. Facilities of good residence and conveyance. Peaceful dealings in the domain of working.

(V) Very cheerful nature. Children bright and beautiful. Very famous. Interest in fine arts. Gets ample help from friends.

(VI) Fearless and dominant. Not afraid of opposition. But has to face impediments in life. Spends money very thoughtfully.

(VIII) Very practical tendency. Beautiful wife. Fine personality. Can adjust with every person everywhere.

(IX) Religious temperament. A lover of justice and fairplay. Interest in music and fine arts. Gets a legacy.

(X) Very brave and aggressive. Good relation with relatives. Gets a very unexpected opportunity of progress. Cordial environment in the place of working. Popular. Religious minded.

(XI) Very thoughtful. Gets unexpected gains. Help from children. May face some hurdles in the beginning of life.

(XII) Very thoughtful. May travel extensively. May have some danger of litigation and opposition.

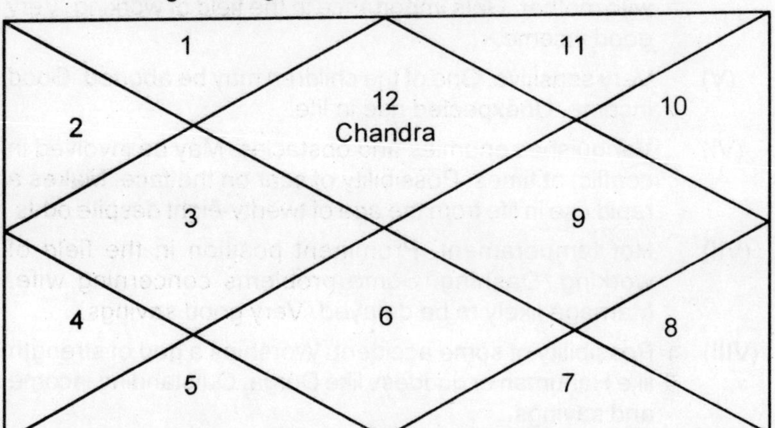

Positions of Mangal in Meena Lagna

House	Effects
(I)	Flies in anger at slight provocation. Some problems with wife. Wealthy. Fortunate. Gets good success from the age of twenty.
(II)	Great savings. Money may come from land or property dealings. Good rise in life from the age of twenty-eight. Energetic and has a sense of self-respect.
(III)	Some difference of opinion with brothers. Gets a prominent position in the place of working. Active and fearless.
(IV)	Some problems concerning home. Non-smooth relations with mother. Gets importance in the field of working. Very good income.
(V)	Very sensitive. One of the children may be aborted. Good income. Unexpected rise in life.
(VI)	Vanquishes enemies and obstacles. May be involved in conflict at times. Possibility of scar on the face. Makes a rapid rise in life from the age of twenty-eight despite odds.
(VII)	Hot temperament. Prominent position in the field of working. Dashing. Some problems concerning wife. Marriage likely to be delayed. Very good savings.
(VIII)	Possibility of some accident. Worships a god of strength like Hanuman or goddess like Durga. Outstanding income and savings.

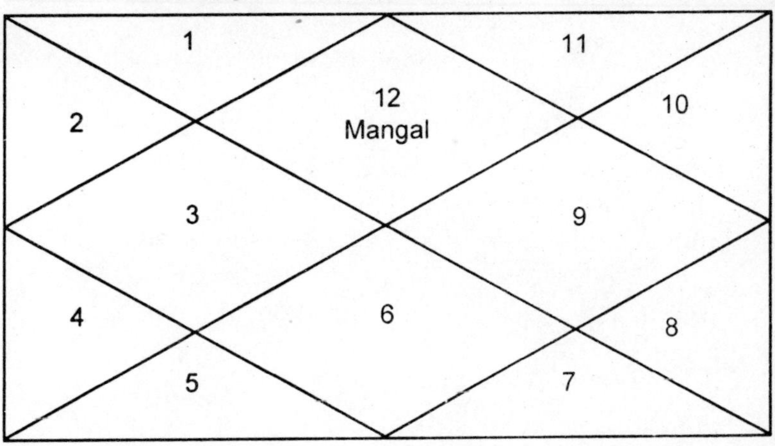

(IX) Very fortunate and dashing. Capacity of outshining others in competition. Maintains self-dignity. Spends heavily.

(X) Very important position in the place of working. Enjoys facilities of good residence and vehicles but experiences some dissatisfaction on the home front. Difference of opinion with children.

(XI) Outstanding income and savings. Differences with children. Danger of abortion of a child. Overcomes opposition and impediments.

(XII) May get good response from friends of foreign origin. Spends money freely. Overcomes opposition and impediments. Some problems concerning wife.

Positions of Shukra in Meena Lagna

House	Effects
(I)	Extremely charming personality. Wife too beautiful. Problems of health.
(II)	Good family environment. Sweet speech excepting the occasions of being angry. Materialistic outlook.
(III)	Good relations with brothers. Active. Diplomatic. Sweet tongued.
(IV)	Home full of facilities like good residential house and vehicles. Satisfaction from home. Smooth sailing in the field of work.
(V)	Girl progeny more in number. Materialistic philosophy. May be helped by girl friends.
(VI)	Deals with opposition in a diplomatic manner. Spends heavily on luxuries. Attempts of betterment likely to be failures. May enjoy material life.
(VII)	Good personality. Danger of health problems. May not have satisfactory conjugal life.
(VIII)	Faith in the ideal of 'eat, drink and be merry'. Difficulties in making savings.
(IX)	Very active. Makes successful attempts for material betterment. Good relations with sisters.

(X) Smooth sailing in the field of working. Happy domestic life. May get some help of a female friend in furthering vocational interests.

(XI) Interest in artistic pursuits. May gain through girl friends. Good relations with progeny.

(XII) Happy material life. Likes to spend on luxuries. Believes in leading a very comfortable life.

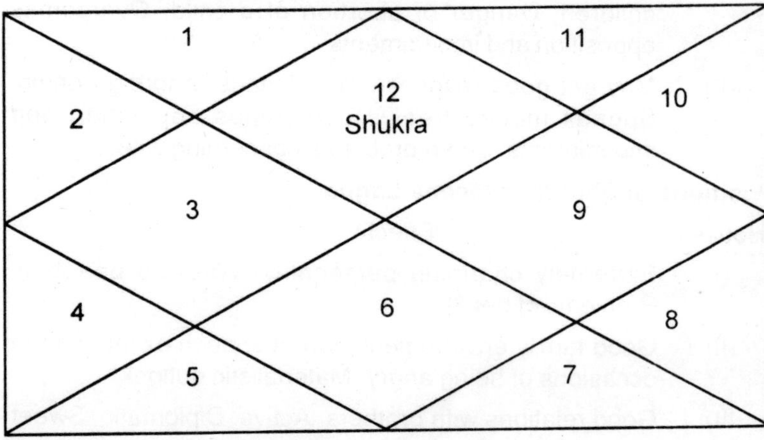

Positions of Budha in Meena Lagna

House Effects

(I) Problems from family and wife. Commercial attitude in life. Some problems of health.

(II) Good education. Happy family life. Sharp intelligence. But speech may not be soft. Outspoken.

(III) Active. Good relations with brothers and sisters. May shine in life after the age of thirty-two.

(IV) Very happy home. All the facilities of residence and conveyances available. Smooth working in the field of action.

(V) Very practical. Good progeny. May think to prosper in the fields of business or journalism.

(VI) Deals with opposition and impediments rather with courage and tact. Spends money very carefully.

(VII) Very successful married life. Good personality. Happy home conditions.

(VIII) Commercial attitude. Good savings. No interest in religion or philosophy. Can prosper in the field of knowledge of economics and commerce.

(IX) Can take risks in life. Dashing. Makes good attempts for success. Gets success after the age of thirty-two.

(X) Very tactful handling of conditions. Commercial outlook. Very practical. Happy domestic conditions.

(XI) Can get good success in the domains of commerce or journalism. Help from wife or marriage brings economic stability.

(XII) May enter into commercial relations with persons of foreign lands. May settle away from birthplace. No deep interest in religion.

Positions of Guru in Meena Lagna

House	Effects
(I)	Very religious minded. Prudent. Good health. Good personality leaning towards fatness. Fortunate and obedient children. Fortunate. Good wife.
(II)	Good savings. Very good rise in life. Free from enemies. Good health. Religious leanings.
(III)	Rise from the age of sixteen or so. Steady income. Obedient wife. Makes rapid progress.
(IV)	Some problems concerning domestic life. Good career. Smooth sailing in the field of activity. Expenses on religious items. Frequent goings to religious places. Aspiration for getting emancipation.
(V)	Unexpected rise in life. Helpful friends. Steady income. Good health. Enjoys reputation.
(VI)	Problem of ill health. Satisfactory condition in the place of working. Liked by fellow workers. Expenses on suspicious items or occurences.
(VII)	Excellent health. Longevity good. Fine personality. Lovable nature. Respected by all. Steady income. Good relations with brothers.

(VIII) Lover of philosophy. Long life. Good savings. Members of family cooperative. Satisfaction of heart in every condition. Expenses on auspicious items.

(IX) Very good rise in life. Bright and fortunate children. Good relations with brothers. A man of self-respect.

(X) Good rise in life. May shine in the field of law, education or religious sermoning. Happy domestic life. Loved even by enemies.

(XI) Earns through right means. Steady income. Helpful friends. Helpful brothers. Helpful children.

(XII) A lover of deep philosophical and knowledge. Deep interest in emancipation. Rightful expenses.

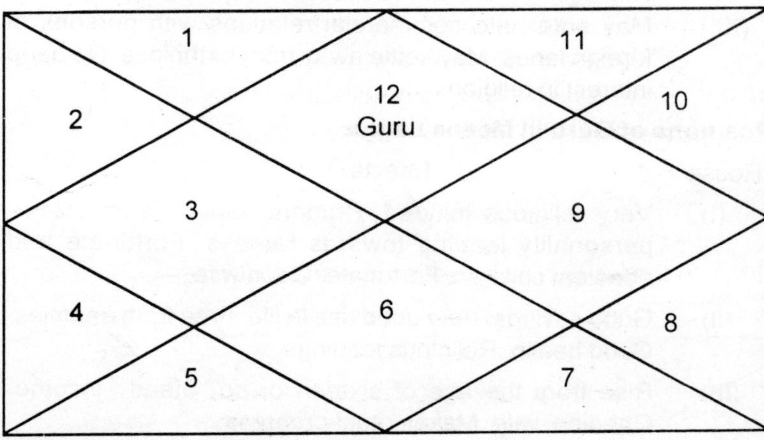

Positions of Shani in Meena Lagna

House Effects

(I) Contemplative mind. Heavy expenses. Non-smooth relations with brothers. Uneasy adjustment with wife. Some obstacles in the field of working.

(II) Excessive expenses. Savings difficult. Dissatisfaction from home. But good income after the age of thirty-six.

(III) Very active. Dissatisfaction from children. Has to struggle for making good progress. Good relations with foreigners. Domestic problems.

(IV) Conflicts in the field of working. Some health problems. Has to deal with enemies and impediments, but conquers them. May settle in some foreign land.

(V) Good income after the age of thirty-six. Income fluctuating. Some problems from children. Dissatisfaction from wife. Saves money with difficulty.

(VI) Reputation on foreign land. Thoughtful. Troubled by enemies, but gives them good fight and wins.

(VII) Late marriage. Obstacles in progress. Some problems of health. Dissatisfaction from home.

(VIII) Long life. Lover of philosophy. Some obstacles in the place of working. Some problems from children.

(IX) Some uneasy relations with brothers. Good income after initial struggles. Defeats enemies.

(X) Some problems from home. Dissatisfied wife. Reputation in foreign lands. Unhelpful partners.

(XI) Very good income after the age of thirty-six. Heavy expenses. Some problems concerning health. Some problems from children.

(XII) A tendency of renunciation. Deep love for meditation and religious pursuits. May get reputation in some foreign land.

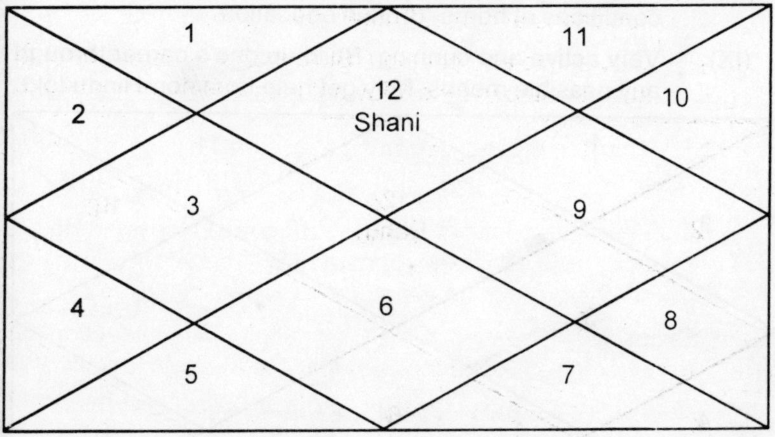

Positions of Rahu in Meena Lagna

House	Effects
(I)	Good personality. Worldly wise. Problems from wife. Some problems concerning health. Faith in Tamasik religion.
(II)	Good savings. But does not care for good or foul means. Hard speech. Good savings after the age of forty-two. Uneasy family atmosphere.
(III)	Very active. Very practical. Very diplomatic. Has many plans for the furtherance of material life. Gets good success after the age of forty-two.
(IV)	Domestic problems. Has all the facilities for domestic prosperity like good residence and conveyances.
(V)	Mind full of various plans and ideas. Some problems from children. Possibility of abortion. Cunning nature.
(VI)	Overcomes obstacles and difficulties through cunningness. Can be successful in the domain of politics.
(VII)	Delay and obstacle in marriage. Difficulty in making adjustment with wife. Marriage may take place out of traditional bonds.
(VIII)	Possibility of an accident. Hard speech. Unsatisfactory conditions at home. Broken education.
(IX)	Very active and cunning. Build up one's career through any possible means. May get help from non-Hindu fold.

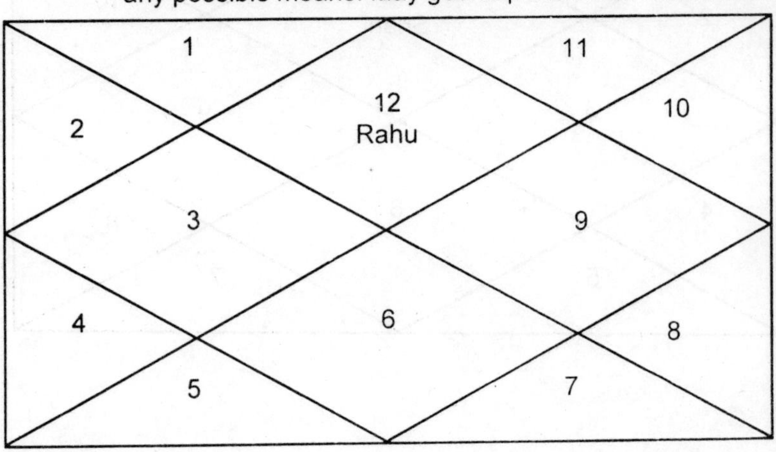

(X) Builds career through struggles. Makes progress through non-moral means too. Rises through cunningness.

(XI) Earns huge wealth after the age of forty-two. May get help from Tamasik forces. Prepared to walk on prohibited ways.

(XII) May settle in some foreign land. Gets help from foreign nationals. Not afraid of competitions. Interest in Tamasik religions.

Positions of Ketu in Meena Lagna

House	Effects
(I)	Good personality. Good nature. Helpful. Some problems from wife. Can adjust with any person.
(II)	Good education. Good environment in family. Soft speech. Cooperative members of family.
(III)	Very active. Gets good success after the age of forty-six. Good relations with brothers.
(IV)	Happy domestic life. Home full of facilities like vehicles and good residence.
(V)	Good and helpful children. Gets unexpected chance of progress. Good income.
(VI)	Wins enemies through tactful dealings. Avoids scuffle. Successful in dealings of the world.

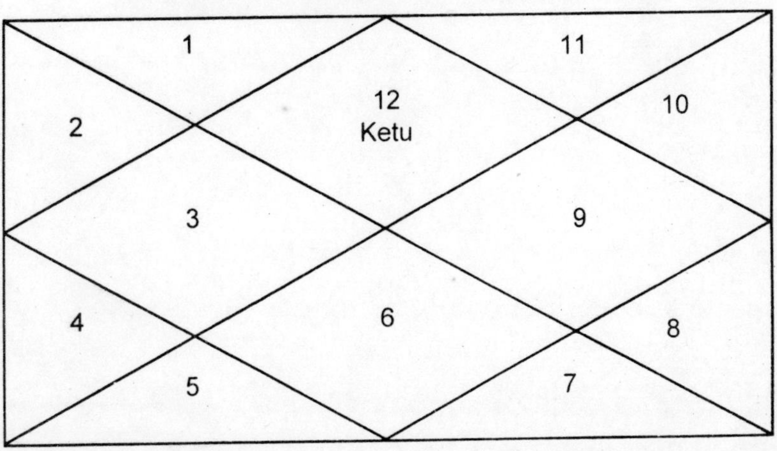

(VII) Good wife. Wife helpful in building career. May prosper through partnership deals.

(VIII) Interest in religious matters. Keen interest in occult sciences. Good longevity. Helpful family.

(IX) Makes good attempts for getting success. Good success possible after the age of forty-six. Little help from brothers.

(X) Good success in diplomatic assignments. Carries out work in the field of activity peacefully. Little comfort from home.

(XI) Unexpected good income after the age of forty-six. May get help from mysterious elements.

(XII) Interest in mystical sciences. May get success in foreign land. May try to get emancipation through Tapasya.

APPENDIX I

SIGNIFICANCE OF SURYA: INDIAN STANDPOINT

Nobody can deny the importance of the sun. It is the sun which dispels darkness and fill's the earth with light; it is the sun which nourishes life; it is the sun which bestows health on man.

From the very Vedic period Indian mind was impressed by the sun. It sang the glory of the dawn in a very telling manner:

"This light is come, amid all lights the fairest: born is the billiant; far-extending brightness.

Night, sent away for Savitor's uprising, hath yielded up a birthplace for the Morning.

The Fair, the Bright is come with her white offspring; to her the Dark one hath resigned her dwelling.

Akin, immortal, following each other, changing their colours, both the heavens move onward.

Common, unending is the Sisters' pathway; taught by the Gods, alternately they travel.

Fair-formed of different hues and yet one-minded. Night and Dawn clash not, neither do they tarry.

Bright leader of glad sounds, our eyes behold her; splendid in hue she hath unclosed the portals.

She, stirring up the world, hath shown us riches; Dawn hath awakened every living creature.

Rich Dawn, she sets afoot the coiled-up sleeper, one for enjoyment, one for health or worship.

Mother of Gods, Aditi's form of glory, ensign of sacrifice, shine forth exalted."

A Brahmin recites the prayer to the Sun rather daily. This prayer is popularly known as the Gayatri Mantra.

ओऽम् भूर्भुवः स्वः तत्सवितुर्वरेण्यं भर्गो देवस्य धीमहि।
धियो यो नः प्रचोदयात्।।

'We meditate upon the excellent splender of the Lord Savitor. May he activate our thoughts.'

The basic assumption underlying Mantra Yoga is that the perceptible universe is made up of only different kinds of vibrations. Vibration is also necessary for the manifestation of consciousness. Savitor is not just the physical sun. It is a concentration of the creative power of the Ultimate Being.

The *Yajnavalkya Samhita* says:

'The Light of lights, the superb light which is hidden in the sun is there in the heart of creatures in the form of consciousness.'

The basic teaching of the Upanishads is that there is only one non-dual Truth and the entire universe is just its manifestation. Therefore the light of the sun is substantially the light of the Supreme. That is why the Lord declares in the Bhagavadgita 'Among the luminaries, I am the bright-eyed Sun'.

The Atharva Veda states about the Rising Sun:

'This spotted deer has come hither, and has sat on the mother earth in the east. And now he is marching forward to his sire the Heaven. He, the Sun, moves about the brilliant spaces, from his out-breath pervades the whole universe. He the bull has looked forth into the heavens. He is the overlord of thirty domains!'

The Sun and the Puranas

Puranas preach the basic spiritual truth in allegorical story forms. They are in fact more popular than the Vedas due to their way of narration.

The Bhagavat Purana is the most important and significant Purana. Its aim is to teach the supreme Truth. *(Satyam parama dhimahi)* The influence of the Purana can be gathered from the fact that Vallabhacharya, one of the important Acharyas of Indian philosophy, gave it as much importance as is given to the *Upanishads,* the *Brahma-Sutras* and the *Bhagavadgita.*

The Bhagavata contains the story of the Syamantaka Mani. (X-56) According to the story, Satrajit was a great devotee of Surya.

Lord Surya was pleased by this devotion and gave him a jewel called Syamantaka Mani. When Satrajit put on this Mani, he became as bright as the sun. The Mani was installed in a temple of Satrajit. When worshipped, it would produce a lot of gold every day. Not only gold was produced, the presence of the Mani would not allow any draught, physical obstacle or mental agony to occur.'

दिन दिने स्वर्ग भारानष्टौ स सृजति प्रभो।
दुर्भिक्षमार्ददिष्टानि सर्पा र्धिकाक्ष्धयो अशुभाः।।

Thus, worship of the Sun was supposed to be a guarantee of peace and prosperity.

A much detailed account of power of Sun-worship has been given by the *Bhavishya Purana*.

The Sun has been described as the Supreme Being:

'You are the eternal God of gods; You are the creator; You are the Lord of the beings.

(adidevo si devanamishvaranam tvamishvarah
adikartasi bhutanam devadeva sanatana)

His wife is Rupa or Sanjha. Yama and Yami are the children of Surya and Rupa. Shani and Tapati are the children of Surya and Chhaya.

Adoration of Surya can destroy every kind of illness as Surya is destroyer of diseases. The skin disease can be cured by the prayer to Surya. Samba, the son of Shri Krishna, had an attack of leprosy due to the curse of Durvasa. But when sought the refuge of Lord Surya, he was completely cured.

The *Padma Purana* contains the story of the King Madreshvara who was the ruler of Madra Desh. He was attacked by leprosy. He was so badly perturbed by the disease that he thought of ending his life. But his people implored him that he must not do so. The state shall be ruined in his absence. He was advised to worship Surya. That worship cured him to the satisfaction of his people.

Surya and the Epics

In India the *Ramayana* and the *Bhagavata Gita* are given utmost respect. These two works have influenced Indian mind to a great extent. In the *Ramayana,* Rama and Sita occupy most important position. Rama is considered the very incarnation of the Supreme

Lord. Rama claims that he belongs to the geneology of Surya. He is Suryavanshi. Rama is considered to be righteousness incarnate.

The *Ramayana* of Valmiki contains what is known as *Adityahridaya Stotra*. Its daily recital brings good luck to the recitor. His enemies are destroyed. He get victory.

Surya is Brahma (the creator), He is Vishnu (the sustainer) and Shiva (the destroyer).

The Mahabharata also talks about the power and influence of Surya. Karna who was a skilful archer was the offspring of Surya from Kunti.

The Bhagavad Gita and Surya

Although the *Bhagavad Gita* is a part of the Mahabharata, it can claim to wield magnificent importance because of its own views. The Gita has been accepted as one of the three most important works of philosophy on which every prominent Acharya wrote his commentary to show that his views are in conformity with the teaching of the Gita. Its perennial philosophy has perennial charm and importance. It is a dialogue between Lord Krishna and Arjuna. No words can describe the significance of the spiritual wisdom enunciated in the Gita. It is interesting to note the statement of Lord Krishna: "I imparted this Yoga first of all to Vivasvana Surya" (IV-1)

"I am the radient sun amongst the lights"

Thus Surya is also the God of spiritual wisdom. In fact the Gayatri Mantra already quoted earlier is a prayer for the grant of spiritual knowledge.

In this context, the following words of Dr Ghurye may be noted:

"The national mind of India yearned for intellectual and spiritual inspiration and urge from divine source as typified by the sun. This yearning for intellectual and spiritual inspiration from the sun has, ever since, remained a characteristic of elite Indians, the descendants of the Rigvedic Indo-Aryans." *(Religious Consciousness*, p. 92)

Surya and Astrology

The science of astronomy and astrology gives utmost importance to Surya. Every horoscope is prepared on the basis of the time of sunrise. Surya is an Atma-karaka *graha*. Generally the owners of the sixth and eighth houses are supposed to be malefic.

But Surya is an exception. Even if it owns 6th or 8th house, its results remain unaffected. Astrology will cease to exist in the absence of Surya and Chandra.

प्रत्यक्षं ज्योतिषं शारमं चन्द्रार्थौ यत्र साक्षिणौ।

Surya and Treatment

Indians have accepted the importance of Surya in the domain of treatment of diseases from the very beginning. We have already noted herein above the views of the Bhavishya and Padma Puranas. The sun-treatment for the skin diseases has often been recommended. Colour therapy is also dependent on the sunlight. This type of treatment adopts the techniques of putting water in bottles of different colours for a specific period. Such water gets curing power.

Sunlight is very effective in curing eyesight defects too.

The technique of palming has proved very useful in increasing eyesight.

The sun is responsible for the seasons. Rains which are very necessary for getting drinking water and the cultivation of grain are dependent on the sunlight alone.

Thus, the Indians have studied the sun from various angles. But it is the beauty of Indian thought that it connects the physical with the metaphysical because as the Isha Upanishad states 'At the heart of all-whatever there is in the universe-abides the Supreme'. The *Bhagavad Gita* too believes that the roots of the universe lie in the Supreme Being. Hence the lustre of the sun is the lustre of the ultimate Being.

Modern science by its very nature of being a material science cannot reach the metaphysical Being. Hence, modern science shall never be able to reach the doorsteps of the attainment of Indian view about Surya.

As Indians however, we can think that Surya is not only a physical being; it is the supreme deity who can be prayed in the following words :

नमांमि देवदेवेशं भूनभावनमव्यवम्।
दिवाकरं शर्वं भानुं मार्तण्डं भरकरं भगम्।।

APPENDIX II

FIXED PERIOD OF MAGADASHAS ACCORDING TO OUR SYSTEM

1. From	Ist year to 6 years	Surya
2. From	7th year to 16 years	Chandra
3. From	17th year to 23 years	Bhauma (Mangal)
4. From	24th years to 44 years	Shukra
5. From	45 years to 62 years	Budha
6. From	63 years to 78 years	Guru
7. From	79 years to 92 years	Shani
8. From	92 onwards	Rahu and Ketu

APPENDIX III

JAPAS FOR THE MITIGATION OF EVILS OF PLANETS

Every graha or planet is a deity, figuratively speaking. If it is not well placed in a horoscope or debilated, the following Japas can mitigate the evil, if performed with faith.

1. For Surya — *Aum Shri Suryay Namah*
2. For Chandra — *Aum Shri Chandraya Namah*
3. For Mangala — *Aum Shri Mangalaya Namah*
4. For Shukra — *Aum Shri Shukraya Namah*
5. For Budha — *Aum Shri Budhaya Namah*
6. For Guru — *Aum Shri Guruve Namah*
7. For Shani — *Aum Shri Shanaye Namah*
8. For Rahu — *Aum Shri Rahave Namah*
9. For Ketu — *Aum Shri Ketave Namah*

If one has deep faith in any Ishta Devata or any favourite deity, one can perform Japa in its name, for example, *Aum Shri Ramaya Namah, Aum Shri Krishnaya Namah* or *Aum Shri Shivaya Namah*.

Faith is important.

It will be better that some Japas are performed daily.

If one has time, one can perform the Japa of all the nine planets. After the conclusion of Japa everyday, one should have this feeling that the deity is pleased and showers its blessings. This feeling is very important.

APPENDIX IV

SOME EXAMPLES ILLUSTRATING THE UTILITY OF THIS WORK

Let us take first the horoscope of our present Prime Minister Shri Atal Bihari Vajpayee.

Astrologers differ as to his Lagna. Some say that it is Tula, some say, it is Vrishchik and some say that it is Mithun.

We need not enter into any controversy here. We can take the position of Surya at the time of his birth and can cast the following horoscope:

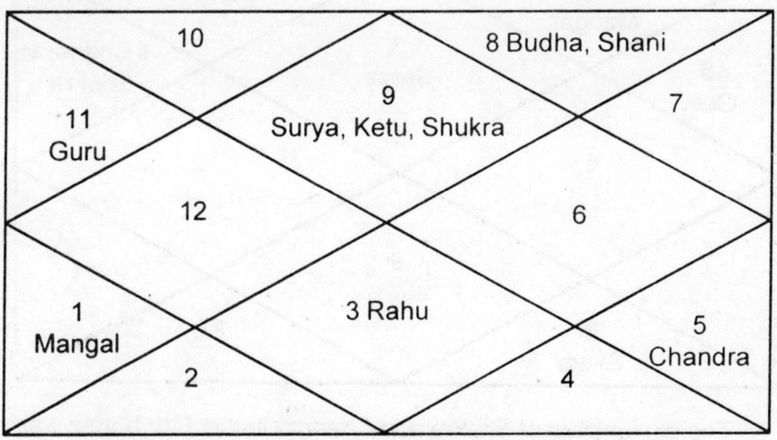

1. Position of Surya in the Lagna makes him very fortunate. The combination of Surya, Shukra and Ketu has given him political skill and success. Surya in Dhanu makes him virtuous.

2. Presence of Rahu in the 7th house and aspects of Lagna planets impel him to remain unmarried.

3. Position of Chandra in Simha and that of Mangal in Mesh have made him courageous. He gave Hydrogen Bomb to India. Without caring for internal or external pressures.

4. From 23 to 43 years he had Shukra Mahadasha. During this period although he did not marry, but he participated in Kavi Sammelanas and composed poems.

At present, i.e., from the age of 63 to 78 he has the Mahadasha of Guru who happens to be the owner of Lagna and 4th houses.

This period has given him the highest position of Prime Minister as well as some moments of sorrow and disgust.

However, the position shall become solid when Guru shall enter Mesha next year.

He shall stay in power despite the attempts to overthrow him by his opponents.

Late Pandit Onkarnath Thakur

He was an outstanding singer of his time. His horoscope from the Surya Lagna is as stated herein below:

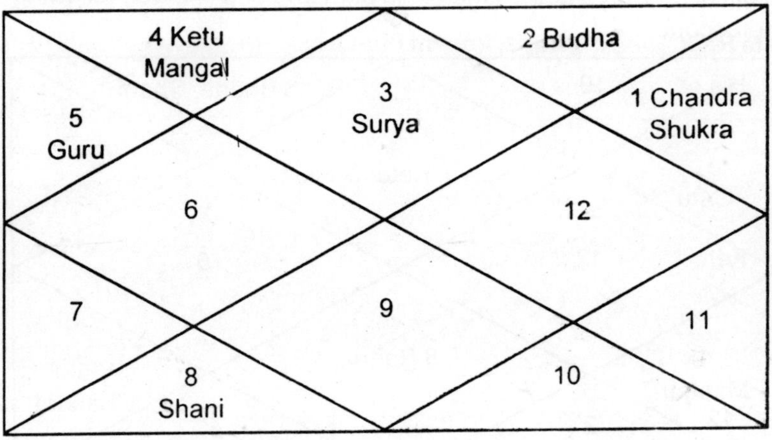

The conjunction of Shukra and Chandra in the 11th house was responsible for his outstanding gift of singing. Moreover it was aspected by Guru. This gave additional strength to the gift.

Dr. Shankar Dayal Sharma, Ex President of India:

His horoscope is stated herein below:

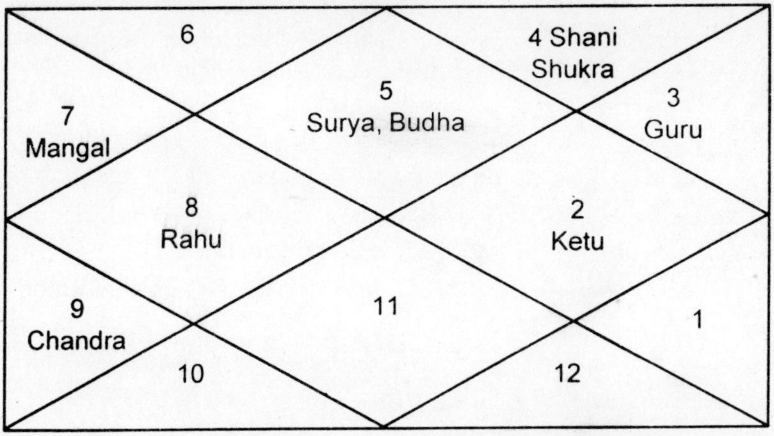

Excellent combination of Surya and Budha in the Lagna gave him important positions. The aspect of Mangal, the lord of fortune on 9th house too gave him important positions.

Late Rajkapoor, the well-known Film Actor, Producer, Director:

His horoscope is stated herein below:

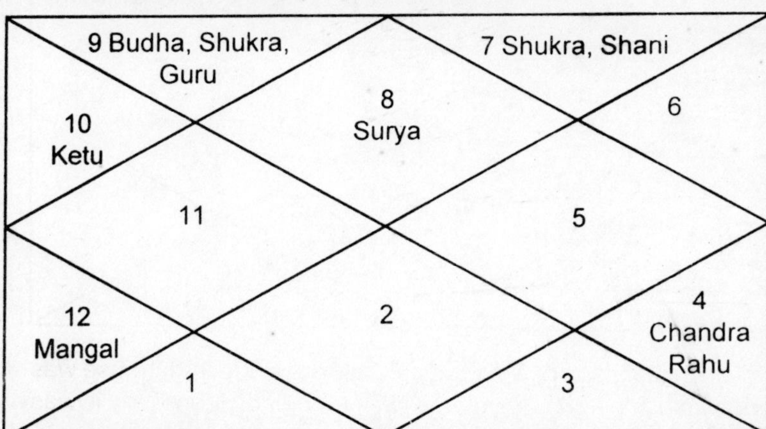

The combination of Chandra and Rahu in the house, the presence of Surya the lord of 10th house in the Lagna, and conjunction of Shani and Shukra in Tula Rashi were responsible for his fame and success.

APPENDIX V

DR. SCHUESSLER'S THEORY OF TWELVE SALTS FOR THE TREATMENT OF AILMENTS

The present book is not concerned with the problem of health. And yet a mention of twelve salts may be made for the treatment of ailments. These salts are safe and can be taken without any hesitation for treatment. Even when they are taken in excess, no harm is done. As these salts are supposed to be connected with birth dates too, their details are being given for the benefit of persons interested in it :

1.	21st March to 20th April	Calcaria Phos
2.	21st April to 20th May	Natrum Sulf
3.	21st May to 20th June	Kalimur
4.	21st June to 20th July	Calcaria Flour
5.	21st July to 21st August	Mag Phos
6.	22nd August to 23rd September	Kali Phos
7.	24th September to 23rd October	Kali Sulf
8.	24th October to 22nd November	Calcaria Sulf
9.	23rd November to 20th December	Silicia
10.	21st December to 19th January	Natrum Phos
11.	20th January to 18th February	Natrum Mur
12.	19th February to 20th March	Farum Phos

These are called birthday salts. It is presumed that these salts shall benefit a person born in a specific period.

APPENDIX VI

RASHIS AND THEIR OWNERS

Sl. No.	*Name of the Rashi*	*Number Denoting Rashi*	*Owner*
1.	Mesha	1	Mangala
2.	Vrishabha	2	Shukra
3.	Mithuna	3	Budha
4.	Karka	4	Chandra
5.	Simha	5	Surya
6.	Kanya	6	Budha
7.	Tula	7	Shukra
8.	Vrishchik	8	Mangal
9.	Dhanu	9	Guru
10.	Makara	10	Shani
11.	Kumbha	11	Shani
12.	Meena	12	Guru

Specifications of Houses

I	Ascendant (Lagna)	rules mainly	body
II	Second house	do	riches, speech, right eye
III	Third house	do	brothers and effort
IV	Fourth house	do	mother, domestic condition, happiness
V	Fifth house	do	intelligence, education, progeny
VI	Sixth house	do	diseases, enemies

VII	Seventh house	do	life partner
VIII	Eighth house	do	death
IX	Ninth house	do	fortune, luck
X	Tenth house	do	field of activity
XI	Eleventh house	do	income, friends
XII	Twelfth house	do	expenses, left eye

APPENDIX VII

FAVOURABLE MONTHS AND YEARS FOR EACH LAGNA

Lagna	Months	Years
Mesh Lagna 	When Surya is in Mesha, Mithuna, Simha, Dhanu, Makara or Kumbha	When Guru is in Mesha, Mithuna, Simha, Dhanu, Makara or Kumbha
Vrishabh Lagna 	When Surya is in Karka, Kanya, Makara, Kumbha or Meena	When Shani is in Karka, Kanya, Tula, Makara, Kumbha or Meena
Mithuna Lagna 	When Surya is in Simha, Tula, Dhanu, Kumbha, or Mesha	When Shani is in Mithuna, Simha, Tula, Dhanu, Kumbha or Mesha
Karka Lagna 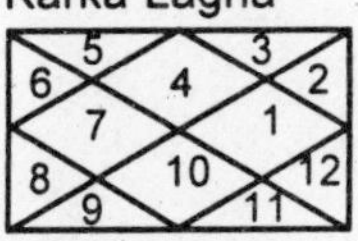	When Surya is in Simha, Dhanu, Mesha, Mithuna or Vrishabha	When Guru is in Mesha, Vrishabha, Karka, Vrishchik, Simha, Tula, Dhanu, or Meena
Simha Lagna 	When Surya is in Simha, Dhanu, Mesha, Mithuna or Vrishabha	When Guru is in Simha, Tula, Dhanu, Kumbha, Mesha, Vrishabha, or Mithuna
Kanya Lagna 	When Surya is in Vrishchika, Kumbha, Mithuna, or Karka	When Guru in Kanya, Tula, Vrishchika, Makara, Meena, Vrishabha, Mithuna or Karka

Tula Lagna

When Surya is in Vrishchika, Dhanu, Kumbha, Mesha, Mithuna, Karka or Simha

When Guru is in Tula, Dhanu, Kumbha, Mesha, Mithuna, Karka or Simha

Vrishchik Lagna

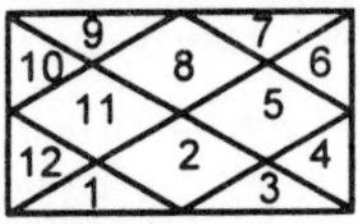

When Surya occupies Dhanu, Makara, Meena, Mesha, Karka, Simha or Kanya Rashis

When Guru occupies Vrishchika, Dhanu, Makara, Meena, Vrishabh, Karka, Simha or Kanya Rashis

Dhanu Lagna

When Surya occupies Kumbha, Mesha, Simha, Kanya or Tula Rashis

When Guru occupies Dhanu, Kumbha, Meena, Mesha, Mithuna, Simha, Kanya or Tula Rashis

Makara Lagna

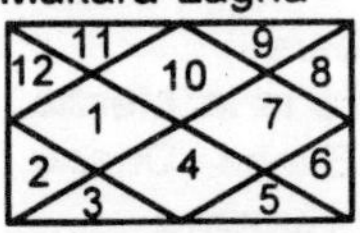

When Surya occupies Meena, Vrishabha, Kanya, Tula or Vrishchika Rashis

When Guru occupies Makara, Meena, Vrishabha Karka, Kanya, Tula or Vrishchika Rashis

Kumbha Lagna

When Surya occupies Mesha, Mithuna, Tula, Vrishchika or Dhanu Rashis

When Guru occupies, Kumbha, Meena, Mesha, Mithuna, Simha, Vrishchika, Tula or Dhanu Rashis

Meena Lagna

When Surya occupies, Mesha, Vrishabha, Simha, Vrishchika, Dhanu or Makara Rashis.

When Guru occupies Meena, Mesha, Vrishabha, Karka, Kanya, Vrishchika, Dhanu or Makara Rashis.

APPENDIX VIII

STAYING PERIODS OF PLANETS IN A RASHI

Name	*Period*
Surya (Sun)	30 days
Chandra (Moon)	54 hours (2¼ days)
Mangal (Mars)	45 days
Budh (Mercury)	30 days
Guru (Jupiter)	12 months
Shukra (Venus)	27 days
Shani (Saturn)	30 months
Rahu (Dragon's head)	18 months
Ketu (Dragon's tail)	18 months

APPENDIX IX

THE SHORTEST DESCRIPTIONS OF PLANETS AND RASHIS

Planets:

Mangal	A brave opposition
Shukra	Tendency to lead luxurious life
Budha	Practical attitude
Chandra	Sentimental tendency
Surya	Courageous bearing
Guru	Religious spirit
Shani	Capacity to bear hardship
Rahu	A tendency of plotting
Ketu	Scoring unruffled victory

Rashis:

Mesha	Readiness to combat
Vrishabha	Hardworking but difficult to subdue if provoked
Mithuna	Capacity of adjustment with environment
Karka	Easily swayed by sentiment and transparent nature
Simha	Courageous and egoistic
Kanya	Very practical
Tula	Love for justice and fairplay
Vrishchika	Picks fault in others and teases them
Dhanu	Ready to fight for spiritual values
Makara	Love for the downtrodden and readiness to suffer
Kumbha	Rarely speaks out the inner thinking and patient
Meena	Simple and adjusting

APPENDIX X

FRIENDSHIPS OF PLANETS

Indian astrology believes that planets are friends, they are enemies or they are indifferent.

Permanent friendship between the planets is as stated herein below:

Sl. No.	*Name of Planet*	*Friends*	*Neutral*	*Enemies*
1.	Surya	Chandra, Mangal, Guru	Budha	Shani, Shukra
2.	Chandra	Surya, Budha	Mangal, Guru, Shani, Shukra	None
3.	Mangal	Guru, Chandra, Surya	Shani, Shukra	Budha
4.	Budha	Surya, Shukra	Shani, Mangal, Guru	Chandra
5.	Guru	Surya, Chandra, Mangal	Guru	Budha, Shukra
6.	Shani	Shukra, Budha	Guru	Mangal, Chandra, Surya

But the entire question of friendship, enemity or indifference should be understood in a suggestive manner.

When planets are friends, they mix well, i.e., they mutually help a person. When they are supposed to be enemies, they retain their characteristic qualities. They do not mix well but present complementary features. When planets are indifferent, what is meant is that the combination does not yield any noteworthy results. The best view is that influence of no planet is totally eclipsed in combination. Their confluence yields a new colour just as the mixture of colours in water produces a new colour.

For example, if there is a combination of Guru and Shani, a person shall have the qualities of these both. Even in a state of oppositions situation remains the same and there is a merger of influences.

APPENDIX XI

ASTROLOGY AND PSYCHOLOGY

Although astrology may be considered to be an occult science, it is not unlinked with psychology. In fact, there appears to be some interconnection between the two.

According to Indian astrology, the universe can be thought as the Cosmic Man (Virata Purusha). This Cosmic Man has nine dominant tendencies called Grahas viz. Surya, Chandra, Mangala, Budha, Guru, Shukra, Shani, Rahu and Ketu. Every human being, a conscious being, is therefore swayed by them in some degree or degrees. In Indian poetry the following nine Rasas (sentiments) have been accepted. They are present in every human being. A sentiment is an organized system of emotional tendency centred around something. It is a permanent tendency to feel an emotion, and lies below the level of consciousness:

1. Shringara (Erotic)
2. Hasya (Funny)
3. Karuna (Compassion)
4. Raudra (Violent)
5. Veera (Brave)
6. Bhayanaka (Terrible)
7. Vibhatsa (Ludicerus)
8. Adbhuta (Bizarre)
9. Shanta (Calm)

The nine planets represent these Rasas.

1. Shringara (shukra), 2. Hasya (Budha), 3. Karuna (Chandra), 4. Raudra (Surya), 5. Veera (Mangala), 6. Bhayanaka (Rahu), 7. Vibhatsa (Ketu), 8. Adbhuta (Shani) and 9. Shanta (Guru).

Thus, every human being is ruled by these sentiments. The domination of a particular tendency is indicated by the strength of a particular planet in the horoscope.

In western psychology McDugall accepts fourteen instincts. But psychologists are not unanimous about the number. Indian view in this Psychology gives much importance to personality. Personality is a harmonious system of physique, temperament, intelligence and character. Woodworth has described personality in the following words: "Personality is total quality of an individual's behaviour as it is revealed in his habits of thought and expression, his thoughts, his attitude and interests, his manner of acting and his personal philosophy of life."

Horoscope reveals the personality of an individual. All the planets placed in the different houses of the horoscope exert an integrated influence in forming an individual's personality. But dominant role is played by the Lagna and the Lagna lord. Thus, Mangala, if happens to be the lord of the Lagna, shall make a person brave. Guru, if it is Lagna lord, shall make a person peaceful. We have already discussed the characteristics of the different planets in this work. Hence, I need not restate them here. It is sufficient to state that a horoscope reveals one's personality to a great extent. Hence, it can be of great use in giving vocational guidance to a person. The significance of a horoscope is thus evident even from the standpoint of psychology apart from its utility in giving predictions.

Index